The Economics of
Crop Insurance and
Disaster Aid

AEI STUDIES IN AGRICULTURAL POLICY

The Economics of Crop Insurance and Disaster Aid

Barry K. Goodwin and
Vincent H. Smith

The AEI Press

Publisher for the American Enterprise Institute

WASHINGTON, D.C.

1995

Available in the United States from the AEI Press, c/o Publisher Resources Inc., 1224 Heil Quaker Blvd., P.O. Box 7001, La Vergne, TN 37086-7001. Distributed outside the United States by arrangement with Eurospan, 3 Henrietta Street, London WC2E 8LU England.

Library of Congress Cataloging-in-Publication Data

Goodwin, Barry K.
 The economics of crop insurance and disater aid / Barry K. Goodwin and Vincent H. Smith.
  p. cm. — (AEI studies in agricultural policy)
  Includes bibliographical references.
  ISBN 0-8447-3908-1 (cloth : alk. paper). — ISBN 0-8447-3909-X (paper : alk. paper)
  1. Insurance, Agricultural—Crops—United States. 2. Disaster relief—United States. 3. Crop losses—United States. I. Smith, Vincent H. II. Title. III. Series.
 HG9968.G66 1995
 368.1'2—dc20   95-16099
                                                   CIP

ISBN 0-8447-3908-1 (alk. paper)
ISBN 0-8447-3909-X (pbk.: alk. paper)

1 3 5 7 9 10 8 6 4 2

The AEI Press
Publisher for the American Enterprise Institute
1150 17th Street, N.W., Washington, D.C. 20036

Printed in the United States of America

Contents

7 CONCLUSION   125

LIST OF TABLES

LIST OF FIGURES

Foreword

The Economics of Crop Insurance and Disaster Aid, by Barry K. Goodwin and Vincent H. Smith, is one of eight in a series devoted to agricultural policy reform published by the American Enterprise Institute. AEI has a long tradition of contributing to the effort to understand and improve agricultural policy. AEI published books of essays before the 1977, 1981, and 1985 farm bills.

Agricultural policy has increasingly become part of the general policy debate. Whether the topic is trade policy, deregulation, or budget deficits, the same forces that affect other government programs are shaping farm policy discussions. It is fitting then for the AEI Studies in Agricultural Policy to deal with these issues with the same tools and approaches applied to other economic and social topics.

Periodic farm bills (along with budget acts) remain the principal vehicles for policy changes related to agriculture, food, and other rural issues. The 1990 farm legislation expires in 1995, and in recognition of the opportunity presented by the national debate surrounding the 1995 farm bill, the American Enterprise Institute has launched a major research project. The new farm bill will allow policy makers to bring agriculture more in line with market realities. The AEI studies were intended to capitalize on that important opportunity.

The AEI project includes studies on eight related topics prepared by recognized policy experts. Each study investigates the public rationale for government's role with respect to several agricultural issues. The authors have developed evidence on the effects of recent policies and analyzed alternatives. Most research was carried out in 1994, and draft reports were discussed at a policy research workshop held in Washington, D.C., November 3–4, 1994. The individual topics include investigation of

- the rationale for and consequences of farm programs in general
- specific reforms of current farm programs appropriate for 1995, including analysis of individual programs for grains, milk, cotton, and sugar, among others
- agricultural trade policy for commodities in the context of recent multilateral trade agreements, with attention both to long-run goals of free trade and to intermediate steps
- crop insurance and disaster aid policy
- the government's role in conservation of natural resources and the environmental consequences of farm programs
- farm credit policy, including analysis of both subsidy and regulation
- food safety policy
- the role of public R & D policy for agriculture, what parts of the research portfolio should be subsidized, and how the payoff to publicly supported science can be improved through better policy

Crop insurance legislation passed in the last Congress is already showing signs of wear. The present volume by Barry Goodwin and Vincent Smith shows why marginal reforms around the edges are not sufficient. Fundamental concerns about who buys subsidized crop insurance and how the insurance affects incentives of farm participants must be addressed. According to the authors, facing these problems may raise the question whether it is feasible to design a functioning policy of government-backed crop insurance and disaster aid. The evidence of past failures does little to bolster confidence in current reforms.

Selected government policy may be helpful in allowing agriculture to become more efficient and effective. Unfortunately, most agricultural policy in the United States fails in that respect. In many ways, the policies of the past six decades have been counterproductive and counter to productivity. Now, in the final few years of the twentieth century, flaws in policies developed decades ago are finally becoming so obvious that farm policy observers and participants are willing to consider even eliminating many traditional subsidies and regulations. In the current context, another round of minor fixes is now seen as insufficient.

In 1995, Congress seems ready to ask tough questions about agricultural policy. How much reform is forthcoming, however, and which specific changes will be accomplished are not settled and depend on the information and analysis available to help guide the process. Understanding the consequences of alternative public policies is important. The AEI Studies in Agricultural Policy are designed to aid the process now and for the future by improving the knowledge base on which public policy is built.

CHRISTOPHER DeMUTH
American Enterprise Institute
for Public Policy Research

Acknowledgments

Any major academic enterprise involves many more people than the authors of the text. We owe particular debts of thanks to Dan Sumner, whose support was invaluable, and Joe Glauber, whose enthusiasm for this project provided us with great encouragement and whose intellectual contributions saved us from many egregious errors. We also would like to thank Julian Alston, Joe Atwood, Alan Baquet, Art Barnaby, Steve Blank, Keith Coble, Hyunok Lee, Michelle Mara, Mario Miranda, and Jerry Skees, all of whom provided us with useful insights. We would like to thank Sheila Smith for her patience, thoroughness, and cheerfulness as she helped us put the manuscript together for publication. Finally, senior authorship is not assigned.

The Economics of Crop Insurance and Disaster Aid

1
Introduction

Popular wisdom maintains that agriculture is subject to greater risk and uncertainty than most other sectors of the economy and therefore is more in need of government disaster assistance than most other sectors. The fundamental reason for the presumption that agriculture is a risky business is the inherent nature of agricultural production. Agricultural production is subject to unpredictable, random shocks caused by weather events, pest damages, and other natural disasters such as fire. The relative frequency of such events as widespread droughts and flooding is believed to generate significant yield instability. The randomness of supply, coupled with inelastic demand for many agricultural products, leads to price movements that are perceived to be more volatile for farm products than those commonly experienced in other sectors of the economy.

In addition, most farm enterprises are small firms operating with small asset bases, despite a measurable trend toward larger farming enterprises over the past fifty years. Large fixed costs are associated with U.S. farming because of the capital-intensive or land-intensive characteristics of U.S. agricultural production techniques. As a result, agricultural producers are often believed to be highly leveraged against their small asset bases even though, in fact, the average debt-to-asset ratio in the U.S. agricultural sector of less than 0.2 is very low. Low asset bases and high debt levels would certainly create problems for the feasibility of self-insurance by farms against production risks. Many businesses with small asset bases in other sectors of the economy, however, are also dependent on borrowed capital, are highly leveraged, and face potentially ruinous shifts in prices, often as a result of volatility of demand.

Government Programs

Historically, policy makers have repeatedly justified a wide range of government programs providing farmers with income transfers, stable prices, and stable incomes on the basis of the instability of agricultural production and agricultural prices. Most programs are intended to support and stabilize agricultural prices and incomes. Two programs, however, federal crop insurance and legisled disaster relief payments, specifically target protection for producers against the risk of reduced yields and have played an increasingly important role in U.S. domestic agricultural policy.

In 1938, legislative efforts to protect producers against yield risks resulted in the Crop Insurance Act. The 1938 act provided protection against crop losses from any (multiple) risks. The program was briefly discontinued between 1943 and 1945 but has generally maintained many of its original features over the past fifty years. Over its entire history, the program has suffered from low participation and high losses. Under the current program, producers have the opportunity to insure their crops at guaranteed yield levels of 50 to 75 percent of their average yields. The insurance is marketed primarily through private insurance companies, although at times producers have also been able to purchase insurance through county Agricultural Stabilization and Conservation Service (ASCS) offices of the U.S. Department of Agriculture. The private insurance companies are reimbursed for a share of their operating expenses and actuarial losses. To encourage participation, since 1980 the government has provided significant premium subsidies to producers. These subsidies have averaged about 25 percent of total premiums.

In addition to multiple-peril crop insurance, more recent legislative initiatives to protect producers against yield risks have included ad hoc disaster relief payment programs. Government provisions for disaster relief have been in existence since the nineteenth century, with most disaster payments for the reconstruction of public facilities damaged by natural disasters. In 1949, Congress established the Farmers Home Administration emergency disaster loan program. This program offered low-interest loans to agricultural producers who suffered significant yield losses. Agricultural disaster payments were initially established in the early 1970s. Producers who suffered catastrophic losses (typically, yields below 50 to 60 percent of normal) were reimbursed for their losses through direct payments from the government. Much of the impetus that led to the introduction and persistence of disaster relief programs is reflected in low participation rates for the concomitant crop insurance program. Producers had the option of insuring against catastrophic yield losses by purchasing protection through the federal crop insurance program. A majority of producers, however, chose not to buy federal crop insurance. When widespread losses occurred in the 1970s and 1980s, constituents from agricultural states, made up largely of uninsured producers, successfully lobbied their representatives for direct disaster payments. As disaster relief payments became institutionalized, the disaster program became analogous to insurance provided free of charge to producers. As a result, incentives to participate in the voluntary federal crop insurance program were further diminished.

Recent Crop Insurance and Disaster Relief Programs

Table 1–1 contains summary statistics for recent (1985–1993) U.S. crop insurance and disaster relief programs. In most years, about 50 million acres of U.S. crop acreage have been insured, while total insurable crop acreage has averaged about 250 million acres. This number corresponds to a typical participation rate of about 20 percent. The 1989 and 1990 crop years were notable for their high participation levels. Much of this participation was mandatory, however. Severe drought in 1988 and 1989 led to significant disaster payments in 1989 and 1990. A condition of receiving these payments was participation in the crop insurance program in the following year. An examination of indemnity payments and producer premiums shows that, in every year, indemnity outlays far exceeded premiums collected from farmers. If direct premium subsidies are included as a part of indemnity payments, the annual average loss ratio (the ratio of outlays to funds collected) for the program is 2.04. This means that, on average, producers received $2.04 in indemnities for every dollar of premiums they paid, an implied average annual rate of return of 104 percent on the dollars they invested in the program.

Over the same period, nearly $9 billion were distributed in the form of ASCS ad hoc disaster relief payments. These payments do not include emergency loan payment defaults of the Farmers Home Administration, which totaled nearly $11 billion over the same period. Thus, the sum of net taxpayer outlays for the three agricultural disaster assistance programs (crop insurance, emergency Farmers Home Administration loans, and ASCS disaster relief payments) amounted to more than

TABLE 1-1
SUMMARY STATISTICS FOR U.S. DISASTER RELIEF AND CROP INSURANCE PROGRAMS, 1985–1993
(millions of dollars)

Year	Insured Acres	Total Premiums Paid ($)	Government Subsidies Paid ($)	Indemnities Paid ($)	Net Outlays[a] ($)	Implied Loss Ratio[b]	ASCS Disaster Payments (4)	Disaster Payment Recipients (thousands of $)
1985	47.50	339.73	100.11	683.17	443.55	2.01	-0.06	0.06
1986	47.82	291.65	88.10	615.70	412.15	2.11	1.87	7.72
1987	48.25	277.51	87.62	369.80	179.92	1.33	557.16	122.54
1988	54.68	328.40	107.99	1,067.56	847.15	3.25	1,319.08	249.51
1989	100.47	613.11	206.28	1,215.22	808.39	1.98	2,740.22	658.10
1990	101.31	618.48	214.39	971.05	566.96	1.57	849.94	255.78
1991	82.36	547.01	190.10	956.40	599.49	1.75	734.69	243.61
1992	83.08	561.96	196.67	921.36	556.07	1.64	1,112.66	461.03
1993	83.74	555.64	199.95	1,647.59	1,291.90	2.97	1,521.24	325.31
Average	72.14	459.28	154.58	938.65	633.95	2.04	981.87	257.48
Total	649.22	4,133.49	1,391.22	8,447.85	5,705.58	2.04	8,836.80	1,283.97

a. Outlays include government premium subsidies and indemnity payments.
b. Loss ratios are ratio of total outlays to premiums collected. The loss ratios thus include premium subsidies.
SOURCE: Environmental Working Group, Agricultural Disaster Assistance Database.

$25 billion between 1985 and 1993 at an annual average cost of about $3.1 billion. Most of these outlays were payments to compensate farmers for yield shortfalls.

One important question raised by such large transfers from taxpayers to agricultural producers is whether any economic efficiency rationale or equity argument justifies such welfare reallocations. Agriculture has been afforded special protection on the grounds that the business of farming is riskier than other business enterprises. In addition, farmers have been assumed to be more dependent on borrowed funds, making them more vulnerable to random production shocks. Both of these assumptions have some factual support. Crop yields are subject to a wide variety of natural hazards, and many farmers (especially new entrants into the industry) are highly leveraged. Nevertheless, other sectors of the economy are also subject to randomness and, in many cases, also depend heavily on borrowed funds. As a result, firms in these sectors (for example, retailing and computer software) experience much higher failure rates than farming enterprises do. Moreover, these sectors of the economy (such as retailing) have not generally been as successful as agricultural producers in securing public protection from production and other income shocks.

Problems of Measuring Risk

Given the popular wisdom, a natural question is why private insurance markets have failed to develop comprehensive contracts that protect farmers against multiple perils. Extensive insurance markets exist for a wide range of risks in the private sector.[1] Standard economic argu-

1. The insurance exchange at Lloyd's of London provides insurance against almost any imaginable risk up to and including bets on whether the Loch Ness monster exists (Borch 1982a). Such an insurance exchange provides diversification of risks across entirely different agents in activities around the world.

ments for government intervention usually involve the proposition that some form of market failure exists. A primary function of private insurance markets is to spread nonsystemic risks among a pool of risk-averse agents. If risks are nonsystemic (uncorrelated among agents), then the insurance provider diversifies the risks of individual losses across the insurance pool. If risks are systemic such that insured agents suffer losses together, however, diversification of risks is impossible, and the insurance provider may be unable to cover losses in a given year.

In the case of multiple-peril or all-risk crop insurance, it is usually argued that the systemic risks associated with crop failures make diversification and risk pooling difficult on a scale feasible for most private insurance markets. This argument follows from the fact that large crop losses, triggered by drought, flooding, or other natural disaster, usually affect agricultural production over a large geographic area. Natural disasters that lead to crop failures are assumed to create loss exposures too large for standard private insurance companies to manage. Thus, the government has to accept the role of reinsurer of last resort on the basis of a general market failure (nondiversifiable systemic risk) that prohibits the purely private insurance contracts.

Although a significant proportion of the risks associated with insuring crops may be systemic within the U.S. agricultural sector, this fact does not imply that these risks are not diversifiable. A larger array of reinsurance options exists in both national and international insurance markets. Such markets are easily able to permit enough diversification to spread risks that appear to be systemic to individual markets across a wider range of activities and markets.

Problems with identifying and measuring risks may be more fundamental to the prohibition of private insurance contracts than arguments that appeal to the lack of risk-pooling opportunities. In particular, as we show in chapter 2 and chapter 4, insuring against multiple crop risks presents formidable challenges in the construction of insurance contracts and the formulation of insurance premium rates. The development of actuarially sound insurance contracts requires insurance providers to obtain accurate measures of loss risks. If agents have more information about their risk of loss than do insurance providers, as is often the case, markets become distorted and participation becomes skewed. This is the classic problem of *adverse selection.* In the absence of an accurate means for measuring individual risks, insurance providers may set rates according to some average, measurable level of risk. In this event, low-risk agents are overcharged for insurance, and high-risk agents are undercharged. Participation levels are skewed toward the riskier agents, the risk of the insurance pool rises, and indemnity payouts rise. In these circumstances, insurance contracts may fail if losses are sufficiently large.

A further problem facing insurance providers is the monitoring of individuals' actions. If insurance providers cannot monitor agents' actions and if agents alter their behavior after buying insurance to affect their likelihood of collecting indemnities, the problem of *moral hazard* may threaten the actuarial soundness of an insurance program.

Adverse selection and moral hazard may present major obstacles to the formation of private crop insurance markets. Because of a general lack of producer-specific risk information, yield risk may be particularly hard to measure. Further, monitoring agents' self-protection against losses may also be problematic. The historical experience of the federal crop insurance program has reflected these difficulties. Whether private multiple-peril crop insurance markets would develop in the absence of the federal program is unclear. Such markets, however, would almost certainly have much lower participation rates and therefore would provide insurance coverage for a much smaller proportion of the agricultural sector. Private markets would not be able to tolerate repeated loss ratios above 1, and as participation in an insurance program is heavily influenced by expected returns to insurance, the lower loss ratios required by private insurers would almost certainly lower expected returns to producers and reduce participation. Only if private markets were able to offer coverage at much lower insurance rates (because of some unseen efficiency gains) would one expect participation to remain close to current levels. Given that the government currently subsidizes about half the indemnities paid to farmers, this possibility seems unlikely.

Measurement of specific risks for perils such as fire and hail appears to be more straightforward. In addition, these specific risks are likely to be less systemic and more immediately diversifiable within the insured pool of farmers than the risks associated with multiple-peril coverage. Private crop insurance markets for fire and hail do exist. Participation by producers in these programs is typically very small when compared with the federal program. The existence of such programs, however, may indicate the range of alternatives for crop insurance that would likely be available in the absence of federal multiple-peril coverage.

Reasons for Protection of Agriculture

Other views on the fundamental reasons for the protection of agriculture have emerged in the political economy literature in recent years. Becker's (1983) seminal work revealed that support was sensitive to factors related to the costs and efficiency of generating political influence. Less concentrated pressure groups cannot focus support and are less successful in generating government assistance. In general, pressure groups provide incentives in the form of campaign contributions or votes to politicians who supply policy-generated income transfers to ensure the continued political support of their constituency. In

9

this context, political considerations lead to a demand for support, while the economic costs of generating such support constrain the supply side. Gardner (1987) examined the fundamental causes of U.S. farm commodity programs in this framework. His work revealed that farm programs are mechanisms for redistributing welfare from taxpayers to agricultural producers. He found that government support for individual commodities was related to the costs of generating political pressure. In particular, he found that support was sensitive to the size of the producer group and that support fell as geographic dispersion of production increased.

These concepts easily extend to a wider consideration of agriculture's role in the economy. For many commodities, the geographical concentration of production creates strong incentives for representatives to secure support. The number of agricultural producers relative to consumers of agricultural products is small. Hence, small taxes or distortions that are borne by consumers of agricultural products or taxpayers translate into large benefits for individual producers. As a result, agricultural protection is an efficient way for elected representatives from agricultural regions to secure support for their constituents. Such support is not unique to the agricultural sector. Other industries in which firms have clearly defined common interests and potential benefits are highly concentrated have also benefited from government programs that redistribute welfare to producers.[2]

According to the empirical evidence, the benefits of the federal crop insurance program and ASCS disaster relief programs are concentrated among a small number of producers. The Environmental Working Group's data-

2. For example, both the U.S. automobile industry and—in the 1960s and 1970s—the U.S. steel industry have received substantial benefits as a result of restrictive trade policies, with substantial adverse effects on the welfare of U.S. consumers.

base (Hoffman et al. 1994) showed that, when districts are ranked according to total indemnity and disaster relief payments, the top ten U.S. congressional districts accounted for over 46 percent of the total taxpayer losses suffered by the federal crop insurance program between 1985 and 1993.

They also reported that the top five congressional districts (for each crop) accounted for roughly 67 percent of all wheat losses, 86 percent of all cotton losses, 41 percent of all corn losses, 97 percent of all peanut losses, and 35 percent of all soybean losses. Benefits from ASCS disaster relief programs have also been heavily concentrated in a small number of congressional districts; the top ten congressional districts accounted for 36 percent of all disaster assistance. Thus, the empirical evidence supports the view that programs that protect yields against risk are mechanisms for redistributing economic welfare from taxpayers to agricultural producers to garner political support for politicians.

To determine whether the purpose of federal crop insurance and other disaster relief programs is to transfer income to farmers or to remedy some forms of market failure, if such programs are politically viable, we must address a second fundamental issue: how disaster aid to farmers can be provided at the lowest possible economic cost to the rest of the economy. Both the major issues raised in this section—whether there is any economic efficiency rationale or equity argument for disaster aid programs and which disaster aid program transfers income to farmers at the lowest possible economic cost—are central to any debate about these programs. As such, they form the core around which we focus our discussion.

In this volume, we examine current federal crop insurance and disaster relief programs for agriculture. We describe the current structure of these programs and provide a historical review of their legislative development. We also review the theoretical and empirical bodies of research that address issues of central importance to the crop insurance and disaster relief programs. Finally, we describe and examine the strengths and weakness of alternatives to the current programs.

2
Current Crop Insurance and Disaster Payment Programs

The current policy mixture of federal multiple-peril crop insurance (MPCI), area-yield insurance, and disaster relief programs is quite complex and, as a result of legislative initiatives for crop insurance reform, is in a state of flux. This chapter provides a comprehensive description of these programs and how they are implemented. The rating procedures used to determine premiums for MPCI contracts receive particular attention because these procedures, which take no account of information on the variability of individual farm yields, are an important reason for the adverse-selection problems and high loss ratios that the program has experienced. Similarly, the appropriateness of current rating procedures for area-yield insurance programs is investigated. In addition, the effects of readily available ad hoc disaster payments (in effect, free crop insurance) on participation in the MPCI program (paid insurance) are examined. Finally, we describe the major provisions of the 1994 Crop Insurance Reform Act that is intended to replace ad hoc disaster relief bills with almost universal catastrophic insurance coverage.

13

Operational Characteristics of the Multiple-Peril Crop Insurance Program

Under the 1995 federal crop insurance program for most field crops, producers are able to select from three guaranteed yield levels (50, 65, or 75 percent of their insurable yield) and from a range of guaranteed price levels. Price election levels are determined from the Federal Crop Insurance Corporation (FCIC) forecasts of expected prices. The top price election level is set at 90–100 percent of the expected market price. Before 1994, three price election levels were available for most crops. Recent program changes under the 1994 Crop Insurance Reform Act (CIRA) now allow price elections between 50 and 100 percent of the top price election level. If the producer's yield falls below the elected coverage level, the producer receives an indemnity payment equal to the product of the elected price coverage and the yield shortfall. This yield shortfall is determined by the amount that actual yields fall short of the farm's insured yield.

The per acre premium is determined by the product of the price guarantee, the yield guarantee, FCIC's estimate of the farm's yield, and the premium rate. Under the 1980 act, subsidies were introduced to encourage participation in the program. There was a 30 percent subsidy on the 50 and 65 percent yield guarantees. The subsidy for the 75 percent yield guarantee was equal to the dollar amount of the 65 percent guarantee level. The total premium subsidy has averaged 25 percent since 1985. Because companies are reimbursed for administrative and delivery costs, however, implicit subsidies are somewhat higher. Federal crop insurance is currently available for about fifty different crops.

Determination of Insurable Yields

Accurate determination of the insurable yields of individual farms has been a major obstacle to avoiding adverse selection. Before 1985, insurable yields for a particular farm were determined by average yields in the farm's geographic area. As Skees and Reed (1986) noted, this method exacerbated adverse selection, as farmers whose risks of loss were above the area averages composed an ever-increasing proportion of the insured pool. In an attempt to address this problem, the FCIC revised its determination of insurable yields in 1985 and now uses the actual production history of the farm to determine insurable yields.

Taking the actual production history, the FCIC used the average of the preceding ten years of the farm's production data to determine the insurable yield. If ten years of data were not available, data on program yields from the Agricultural Stabilization and Conservation Service were used. Beginning with the 1994 crop year, producers could qualify for actual production history yields with only four years of production data, although up to ten years of data are used if available. If less than four years of actual data are available, weighted ASCS program yields are used in place of the missing yields.

To qualify for actual production history yields, the producer must have continuous, verifiable production records for the relevant (four–ten) years. To prevent producers with expected yields below the area average from jumping in and out of the program (and thereby losing their actual yield histories), significant penalties are applied to the transition yields used in place of actual production data when such data are not available. If no actual production data are available, producers' insurable yields are set at 65 percent of their individual transitional yields. If three years of yield data are missing, the missing data are replaced with 80 percent of the transitional yield. If two years are missing, 90 percent of the transitional yield is used.[1] If a single year is missing, 100 percent of the transitional yield is used in lieu of the missing observa-

1. A producer's transitional yield is equal to the farm's ASCS program yield multiplied by a "*t*-factor." The *t*-factor is the

tion. In addition, recent changes in FCIC record-keeping procedures make tracking individuals by taxpayer identification numbers more feasible. In past years, farmers with very low expected yields could "lose" their yield histories by switching companies or by purchasing insurance in a partner's name.[2]

Some have argued that the use of a ten-year average to calculate insurable yields may understate actual expected yields, because yields have exhibited an upward trend that would not be captured in a simple arithmetic average. Given the volatility of yields realized in the 1980s and early 1990s, such a trend is difficult to verify. When a longer time series is examined, however, some evidence of such a trend exists. Thus, policies based on insuring 75 percent of the actual production history yield may offer coverage of some smaller proportion (say, 70 percent) of a farmer's expected yield.

Actuarial Practices and the Problem of Adverse Selection

Many view adverse selection as the most significant problem affecting the actuarial soundness of the federal crop insurance program (Miranda 1991). The presence (or absence) of adverse selection is directly related to the extent to which insurance premiums accurately reflect the like-

county average ASCS program yield divided by the National Agricultural Statistics Service county average yield. As the t-factor is typically less than ASCS program yields and lower than expected yields in most cases, transitional yields are typically much smaller than county average yields.

2. These changes in record-keeping practices are the result of provisions in the 1990 Food, Agriculture, Conservation, and Trade Act, which gave the FCIC the authority to collect social security numbers from participants.

lihood of losses. The FCIC adopts a number of assumptions when determining insurance premium rates that may induce adverse selection in the insurance pool. The most basic (though not necessarily the most serious) shortcoming of rate-setting practices is that rates are determined for a relatively large geographic area (the county in which the farm is located). Thus, all individuals with the same average yield in a county pay an identical premium rate (dollars per $100 of liability) for the same crop and practice type.

In the actuarial determination of county-level rates, the FCIC examines several factors. First, the FCIC looks at the twenty-year loss history of a given county and then at the loss-cost ratios for the preceding twenty years.[3] The four largest loss-cost ratios are capped at the level of the fifth-largest ratio. The capped data are grouped into a pool (representing a catastrophic loading factor), which is later spread over the entire state. The capped loss-cost ratios plus the sixteen lowest loss-cost ratios are averaged to obtain a county loss-cost ratio, which is then used to construct an actuarially sound rate for each county. The loss-cost ratios are then smoothed across county lines to soften large differences in the cost of insurance for neighboring farms. The catastrophic loading factor is next spread across the entire state, and rates are adjusted accordingly. The resulting rates are set for a given crop practice (for example, irrigated versus dry-land production) at the county level. The smoothing and loss-spreading practices may induce adverse selection into rates, since they tend to lower rates in high loss-risk counties and raise rates in low loss-risk counties.[4]

3. The loss-cost ratio is given by the ratio of indemnity outlays to total liability.

4. An additional problem, brought to our attention by Dr. Joseph Glauber in private correspondence, is that coverage levels have varied over the past twenty years (for example, before

Rates are next adjusted according to county average yields, as defined by yield data calculated by the National Agricultural Statistics Service (NASS).[5] Rates are adjusted inversely with county average yields. Thus, counties with high average yields realize premium rate discounts relative to counties with low average yields, regardless of actual losses or yield variation.

County rates are spread over a range of average yields by a proportional spanning procedure. Under that procedure, nine discrete risk categories are defined, and rates in each category are inversely adjusted according to the farm's average yield. In this way, farms with higher average yields have lower premium rates. In addition, because of the proportional nature of the discounting, as average yields increase the premium falls at an increasing rate.

A final constraint faced by the FCIC in its actuarial determination of premiums is a legislative restriction that limits the amount that a rate can increase from year to year. In most cases, premium rates may not increase by more than 20 percent from one year to the next. This constraint may reduce the flexibility afforded to the FCIC for eliminating adverse selection through adjustments in premium rates.

Average Yield as an Indicator of Risk

An important assumption implicit in the FCIC's actuarial practices involves the relationship between average yields and the likelihood of loss.[6] Botts and Boles (1957) noted that the FCIC's use of average yields in initial rating as-

1981, producers could not insure at the 75 percent level against yield loss). Thus, the twenty-year series of loss-cost ratios is unlikely to be stationary.

5. The NASS data used to determine rates are updated rather infrequently. In some cases, a lag of five years may occur before yields are updated.

6. Much of the material in this section was summarized from Goodwin (1994).

sumed a constant relationship between mean yields and the variance of yields. Specifically, they noted that the standard deviation of yields is assumed to be one-fourth of the mean of yields (that is, that the coefficient of variation is 25 percent).

Skees and Reed (1986) used yield averages and standard deviations for four relatively small samples collected from corn and soybean farms in Kentucky and Illinois to evaluate the relationship between yield averages and standard deviations. Their results indicated that no strong relationship existed between the mean yield and the standard deviation of yields. They also evaluated the relationship between the coefficient of variation (the ratio of the standard deviation to the average) and the mean of yields. Their results indicated that the coefficient of variation of yields fell as average yields rose, giving support for rate-setting techniques that apply discounts as average yields rise.

A weakness of inferences drawn from such an analysis is that the estimated relationship between average yields and yield variation is of an aggregate (average) nature. Although Skees and Reed do not explicitly report their regression results, the lack of a significant relationship between average yields and the standard deviation of yields suggests that this relationship varies considerably across the farms in their sample. An important point to recognize is that the farms that purchase insurance are not likely to be randomly drawn from this aggregated sample. That is, finding no relationship between the mean and the standard deviation of yields in an aggregate sample (or even an imperfect relationship) suggests the potential for a self-selected subset of the sample to be at one extreme of this relationship. In particular, insured farms will tend to have higher yield variances relative to their mean yields than uninsured farms.

The use of average yields as an indicator of the risk of loss may thus introduce adverse selection into the insurance pool if the relationship between average yields and relative yield variation is not strong. In reality, considerable differences exist in the relationship between average yields and yield variation across different farms. If rates are determined by average yields, farms with high relative variation in yields are likely to be undercharged for their insurance coverage. Conversely, farms with relatively low variation in yields will be overcharged for insurance and will thus be less likely to buy coverage.

Goodwin (1994) examined the relationship between average yields and relative yield variability (measured by the coefficient of variation calculated from historical yields) using historical yield data for a large sample of Kansas farms. His results indicated that the relationship between average yields and yield variability was relatively weak. In particular, R^2s from regressions of the standard deviation and the coefficient of variation for yields on average yields were quite close to zero. This result indicated that average yields explained only a small proportion of the total variance of yields. He also found that relative yield variation, represented by the coefficient of variation on historical yields, was considerably higher for those farms that purchased insurance. The implication of Goodwin's (1994) analysis is that rating practices that base premiums on average yields may represent risks of loss inaccurately and introduce adverse selection into premium rates.

Operational Characteristics of Area-Yield Insurance Programs

The 1990 farm bill allowed the FCIC to test new insurance products on a pilot basis. As a result, in 1993 the FCIC introduced a pilot area-yield crop insurance program for soybeans, called the Group Risk Plan. In the 1994 crop year, as a result of provisions in the 1993 Omnibus Budget Reconciliation Act, the FCIC received a mandate to offer area-yield contracts in over 1,200 counties (one-third of all counties in the United States) for barley, corn, cotton, peanuts, grain sorghum, soybeans, and wheat. It is unclear whether the Group Risk Plan will continue, since only about 11,500 such contracts were sold in 1994 (as compared with hundreds of thousands of MPCI contracts in those counties). Under the 1994 CIRA, however, the FCIC has a mandate to continue to consider offering Group Risk Plan contracts for some crops in some counties.

The Group Risk Plan offers insurance on a county's average yield on the premise that, when the county average yield is low, most farmers in the county will suffer losses (Baquet and Skees 1994).[7] Under the current program, the FCIC forecasts an expected yield for the county using historical data. Farmers may elect a coverage of 70, 75, 80, 85, or 90 percent of the expected average yield. If the actual county yield falls below the elected coverage (that is, the trigger yield), the farm receives indemnities. The indemnity payment is based on the percentage decline below the trigger yield, and the indemnity amount (measured in quantity of crop) is converted into a dollar amount by multiplying the quantity indemnity by a protection level (measured in dollars per unit of output) that is chosen by the farmer. The protection level chosen by the farmer can range from 30 percent to 150 percent of the expected price for the crop.

An example, drawn from Skees (1994), illustrates the operation of the program. Consider a county in which

7. The effectiveness of the Group Risk Plan for an individual farmer is crucially dependent upon how correlated the farm's individual yields are with the county's average yield. Miranda (1991) and Smith et al. (1994) have shown that the protection offered by the program against yield shortfalls is much less effective for farms with low correlations against county averages.

the expected county average yield for a crop is thirty bushels and the expected price of the crop is $5 per bushel. A farmer who selects the 90 percent coverage would receive an indemnity if the average yield for the crop fell below twenty-seven bushels. Suppose a yield of twenty bushels is realized, a 26 percent shortfall ([27-20]/27 = 0.26). If the farmer selected a protection level of 150 percent, the farmer would receive an indemnity of $58, equal to 0.26 x 30 x 1.5 x $5.

Forecasting Expected County Yields and Developing Rates for the Group Risk Programs

Contract development under the program for Group Risk Plans requires measures of two critical policy instruments—an expected yield and a measure of the distribution of actual yields about this expected yield—for premium rates to be constructed.[8] NASS county average yields are the annual time series data used to estimate these parameters. NASS yield data for counties are available only with a two-year lag (for example, yield data for 1991 were not available until 1993), and therefore forecasts must be generated two years into the future.

Current procedures use double exponential smoothing models to provide forecasts of the expected yields using the NASS time series data on historical annual average yields for each county. Exponential smoothing models are in fact out-of-date technologies. Such models typically have an analogous univariate ARIMA (autoregressive integrated moving average)-type specification. Under exponential smoothing, however, parameters are usually not estimated but instead fixed at

8. This section provides a brief review of current FCIC methods for forecasting expected area yields and determining premium rates. A detailed discussion of these procedures is provided by Skees and Black (1993).

predetermined values.[9] The smoothing models are used to develop a series of forecasts (and forecast errors) for each observation. The two-step-ahead (two years ahead) forecast represents the expected yield, and the forecast errors are used to construct premium rates.

Empirical premium rates are constructed as the average shortfall (that is, the average proportional forecast error when actual yields are smaller than forecast yields). These rates are estimated for the 100 percent coverage level, and then the coefficient of variation on the residuals is used with normal curve theory to smooth the rates for lower levels of coverage. A reserve load is added by dividing the rates by 0.9. The rates are then smoothed across county lines using relative acreage of surrounding counties to determine the size of the weights of surrounding counties.

Goodwin and Ker (1994) discuss the limitations of the current procedures for developing premium rates and expected yields in the Group Risk Plan program. In particular, the use of exponential smoothing models that are not fitted explicitly to historical data may be overly simplistic and may result in large inaccuracies in program parameters. As they note, the ad hoc nature of current procedures may induce adverse selection and inaccurate yield predictions.

Current Disaster Payment Programs

Disaster payment programs have been an important part of U.S. agricultural policy throughout the 1970s, 1980s, and early 1990s. Between 1985 and 1993, over $25 billion was spent on direct disaster relief programs, in addition to outlays brought about by excessive losses in the Fed-

9. Typically, a variety of parameter values are explored, and the specification that performs best is chosen for forecasting.

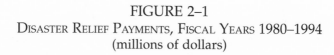

FIGURE 2–1
Disaster Relief Payments, Fiscal Years 1980–1994
(millions of dollars)

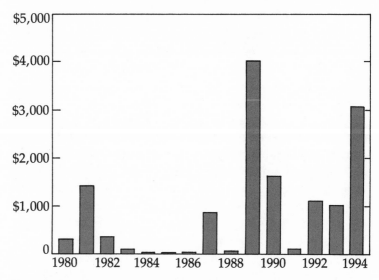

Source: U. S. GAO and Environmental Working Group, Agricultural Disaster Assistance Database.

eral Crop Insurance Program. Figure 2–1 illustrates the incidence and magnitude of direct disaster relief expenditures between 1980 and 1994.

Currently, U.S. disaster relief programs have three main dimensions: direct payments, emergency loans, and federally subsidized crop insurance. Direct payments are administered through a number of individual programs. In particular, of the $6.9 billion administered by ASCS between fiscal years 1980 and 1989, 81 percent was disbursed through crop disaster assistance payments, 14.2 percent was administered through the Emergency Feed Program, 1.5 percent was administered through the Emergency Conservation Program, and small amounts (less than 0.5 percent) were administered through the Forage Assistance and Tree Assistance Programs. Under the

Emergency Loan Program, loans are provided by the Farmers Home Administration at subsidized interest rates to producers who have realized crop and livestock losses as a result of natural disasters. The Emergency Feed Program, established in 1977, reimburses producers who lose at least 40 percent of their feed production because of natural disasters for up to 50 percent of their commercial feed costs. The Emergency Conservation Program, established in 1978, is a cost-share program that provides emergency funds to restore to productive use farmland damaged by natural disasters such as floods. The Emergency Conservation Program also provides funds for emergency water conservation measures during periods of severe drought. The Forage Assistance Program, established in 1988, provides funds on a cost-sharing basis to livestock producers for the reseeding of pastures damaged by the 1988 drought. The program also provided funds for facilitating grazing and haying in the late fall of 1988 and early spring of 1989. The Tree Assistance Program was established in 1988 to provide funds on a cost-sharing basis to tree producers who suffered seedling losses from the 1988 drought. A breakdown of U.S. agricultural disaster relief expenditures among insurance programs, disaster programs, and Farmers Home Administration emergency loans is presented in figure 2–2.

Feedgrain producers have been the primary recipients of disaster relief payments. Figure 2–3 illustrates a breakdown of payments by crops between 1975 and 1986. Corn has been the largest recipient of disaster relief in most years. Wheat and cotton are the second and third largest recipients of disaster payments. Disaster relief benefits are also concentrated in particular geographic areas. A recent report by Hoffman, Campbell, and Cook (1994) showed that the top ten congressional districts for disaster assistance received roughly one-third of the U.S. total for disaster assistance from 1985 to 1993. Their report also showed that 60 percent of total disaster aid from

FIGURE 2–2
Breakdown of U.S. Agricultural Disaster Relief Expenditures, 1985–1993
(millions of dollars)

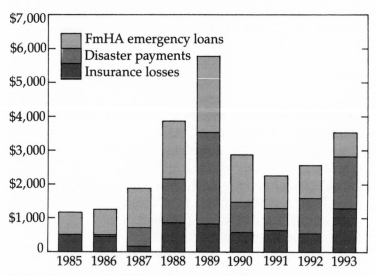

SOURCE: Environmental Working Group, 1994.

1985 to 1993 went to the top ten states: Texas, North Dakota, Minnesota, Kansas, Iowa, Illinois, Wisconsin, South Dakota, Michigan, and Georgia. Finally, their report demonstrated that many farmers receive disaster relief payments nearly every year. In particular, they found that over 107,000 participants in the ASCS disaster payment program received assistance four or more years out of the seven-year period from 1987 to 1993. These producers received a total of $2.55 billion in payments.

Hoffman et al. (1994) concluded that disaster relief programs, including the federal crop insurance program, provide a disproportionate share of benefits to a small number of producers. Further, they suggest that the frequency of payment receipts in certain geographic areas provides evidence that disaster assistance programs of-

FIGURE 2–3

CCC Crop-specific Disaster Relief Payments, 1975–1986
(millions of dollars)

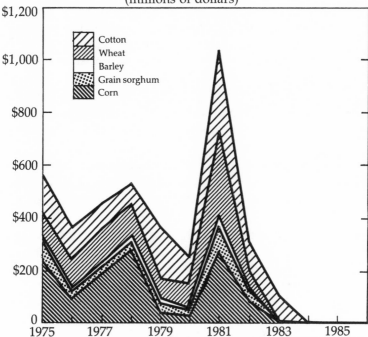

SOURCE: USDA, ASCS.

fer incentives for agricultural production in geographic areas that are especially susceptible to crop losses and would not likely be in agricultural production without disaster assistance. Their claim that such effects are large is questionable and is not supported by any rigorous empirical analysis, but, almost certainly, at the margin some land has been brought into crop production that would otherwise have been allocated for grazing or other uses.

The 1994 Crop Insurance Reform Act

On October 3, 1994, the U.S. Congress passed the 1994 Crop Insurance Reform Act. The provisions of the 1994

27

CIRA will result in several major changes in federal disaster relief programs. The clear intent of the proposed legislation is to reduce federal budgetary outlays on agricultural disaster programs while guaranteeing farmers consistent and reliable access to government support payments when they experience very poor crops.

The 1994 CIRA contains several important innovations. The first set of innovations concerns the introduction of a catastrophic crop insurance contract that is mandatory for all insurable crops on farms that participate directly in government programs. If a farm receives deficiency payments for one or more crops, has a loan from the Farmers Home Administration, or participates in tobacco or peanut programs, the farm must purchase a catastrophic insurance contract for each planted crop for which insurance is available. These "cross-compliance" requirements of the 1994 CIRA will ensure that almost all farmers will participate in the catastrophic component of the crop insurance program.

The catastrophic contract will insure 50 percent of the farm's individual crop at 60 percent of its expected market price at a very low cost. The farmer will be charged a "processing fee" of $50 per crop, but total farm payments for such contracts will be capped at $200 per farm per county and at $600 per farm. Thus, for farms that operate within a single county, catastrophic coverage for additional crops is free when the farm grows more than four crops. In addition, if a farm is designated as a "limited resource" operation (that is, small), then the catastrophic coverage processing fee will be waived. The processing fee is not intended to operate as a premium but to cover costs incurred by agents who sell such contracts. Thus, in the context of the insurance it provides, the catastrophic insurance will be either nearly free or completely free to the farm.

The second set of innovations concerns crops not covered by federal crop insurance programs. Some crops in some counties are simply not covered by an FCIC insurance program. The 1994 CIRA established a noninsured crop disaster assistance program to provide coverage for producers of such crops that is "equivalent to the catastrophic risk protection otherwise available." A "double trigger" will be required before an individual farm receives indemnities under the noninsured crop program. First, the county's yield for the crop must fall below 65 percent of its average yield. Then, in addition, the individual farm must experience yields that are less than 50 percent of its average yield. When both conditions are satisfied, the farm will receive an indemnity equal to 50 percent of its average yield less its actual yield valued at 60 percent of the expected market price. Suppose, for example, a farm grows a crop with an expected price of $5 a bushel and that the farm has a per acre average yield of thirty bushels. If yields in the county are less than 65 percent of the county average and the farm experiences an actual per acre yield of five bushels, then under the noninsured crop program, the farm will receive an indemnity of $30 per acre (equal to (15 - 5) bushels x 0.6 x $5). The intent of the double trigger is to reduce incentives for moral-hazard behavior on the part of individual farms. If farms receive noninsured crop coverage only when countywide yields are low, in most years most farms with only noninsured crop coverage that experience moderately low yields will have little incentive to indulge in behavior that further reduces their actual yields. This coverage is to be provided at no cost to producers.

The third set of innovations concerns premium subsidies and yield and price elections. Under the reform bill, farmers will be able to buy insurance that provides them with yield and price elections similar to those available under the MPCI contracts offered in 1994. If such insurance is purchased, catastrophic coverage is not required. Two important changes have been introduced, however. First, beginning in 1996, farmers in some cases may be able to obtain MPCI contracts with higher, 80 percent, yield elections; that is, a farm may be able to choose a contract that pays an indemnity when the farm's actual yield falls below 80 percent of its average yield.[10] This increase may encourage greater participation in the MPCI program in regions where, for some crops, yields exhibit relatively little variation. For major program crops like corn, these areas include parts of such Corn Belt states as Iowa, Indiana, and Illinois. The change may also be important in encouraging participation among some producers of irrigated crops in such states as California and in stimulating the demand for new MPCI contracts in states that produce fruits and vegetables such as Florida and Massachusetts.

The incentives for participation in MPCI stemming from the increase in the maximum yield election are likely to be enhanced by a subtle but important change in the way in which premiums are subsidized. Under the program as it operated between 1981 and 1994, as we noted above, producers received a 30 percent subsidy on the premiums they paid for contracts with yield elections of 65 percent or less. Farms buying contracts with the higher 75 percent yield election were supposed to pay the full actuarial cost of the additional coverage. Under the 1994 CIRA, farms will receive a lump-sum subsidy equal to that provided under the catastrophic contract for buy-up contracts under which the farm chooses up to a 65 percent yield election and a 100 percent price election, or an equivalent contract. If, however, the farm chooses a yield election above 65 percent at 100 percent price election or purchases an equivalent contract, it receives a larger subsidy equal to the premium established for a 50 percent

10. Under the 1994 CIRA, the FCIC may choose to offer 80 percent yield election contracts but is not required to develop them for all—or, indeed, any—crops in all or any counties.

yield election, 75 percent price election contract. Thus, farms will be able to purchase MPCI contracts with yield elections above 65 percent that offer more heavily subsidized premiums. The combination of higher-yield elections and subsidized premiums for some contracts based on those yield elections may well expand participation in the program but will probably also increase losses (total indemnities less total premiums) because most of the increase in participation will involve new contracts with intentionally subsidized premiums.

A fourth important innovation concerns the procedures by which Congress passes ad hoc agricultural disaster relief bills. Currently, expenditures made under ad hoc disaster relief bills are not counted as part of the federal budget approved by Congress and are not subject to the same fiscal disciplines as most other government expenditures. Under the reform bill, expenditures under these bills would be placed on budget unless majorities above 60 percent prevail in both houses. Thus, typically, disaster payments to farmers would be made under ad hoc disaster relief bills only if cuts were made in other programs. The intent of these innovations is to force Congress to exercise self-discipline in relation to agricultural disaster payments. Given that, as a result of the crop insurance reform bill's cross-compliance provisions, most farms will have nearly free catastrophic insurance coverage, they should not need additional help in times of hardship. Therefore, the crop insurance reform bill has a rider intended to make it costly for Congress to give them that additional help. Happily, that rider probably has some effective teeth.

Conclusion

Since 1981, the federal government has chosen to operate a paid crop insurance program, MPCI, under which farms can be virtually certain of receiving income supplements when crop yields are low. Simultaneously, it has chosen to operate a free crop insurance program, through ad hoc disaster relief measures, under which farms cannot always be certain of receiving income supplements when crop yields are low. The income guarantees provided by the latter program have been more reliable in farm states with relatively large congressional delegations and in such states where participation rates among farmers eligible for crop insurance are relatively low. Ad hoc disaster bills, however, have proved to be costly over the past seven years and have generally been viewed as undercutting participation in, and the financial viability of, the federal MPCI program. The result has been the passage of a crop insurance reform act that provides farmers with almost free mandatory catastrophic crop insurance coverage, expands the subsidized coverage available under the current MPCI program, and limits the ability of Congress to provide ad hoc disaster relief payments. The current and proposed policies are neither new nor the result of pure policy chance. Both federal paid crop insurance and free disaster relief have quite lengthy legislative histories that reveal a great deal about why the current programs exist. These histories are therefore examined in some depth in the next chapter.

3
History of Federal Multiple-Peril Crop Insurance

The current mixture of U.S. agricultural disaster relief programs did not develop in a vacuum, and the programs have had a long and varied history.[1] The first of these programs was initiated in 1938 when Congress enacted legislation to establish the Federal Crop Insurance Corporation as a means of providing all-risk or multiple-peril crop insurance to farmers. The purpose of this insurance was to provide individual farmers with some degree of protection against financial hardship caused by adverse growing conditions that resulted in substantial crop losses. The private sector did offer insurance against risk of crop loss from hail or fire but did not provide general coverage for losses from drought, pests, insect infestations, and the like. Thus, in response to an initiative from President Franklin Roosevelt, Congress developed legislation that shifted the risk of growing crops away from at least some farmers to the taxpayer (Kramer 1983, 181). In this chapter, we first investigate the origins of the provisions of

1. In writing this chapter, we owe a particular debt to Randall Kramer's seminal article, published in 1983, on the history of private crop insurance and the federal crop insurance program over the period 1899 to 1982.

the 1938 Federal Crop Insurance Act, paying particular attention to the rationales for the foundation of a government-subsidized multiple-peril crop insurance program. We then present the history of the program and examine the causes and consequences of major shifts in its structure. Next, we examine the history of the federal government's area-yield crop insurance contract introduced in 1993 as an experimental or pilot program. Finally, we present a brief history of U.S. disaster relief programs.

The Origins of the 1938 Crop Insurance Act

The history of all-risk or multiple-peril crop insurance in the United States began in 1899 when the Realty Revenue Company of Minnesota offered a contract that guaranteed insured wheat farmers a minimum of five dollars per acre for their crop, regardless of the cause of loss. Losses from the Realty Revenue Company contract were so large, however, that the company abandoned the contract after only one year. Between 1900 and 1920, several other companies attempted to offer all-risk crop insurance contracts, but those efforts also foundered rapidly (Valgren 1923). Several reasons for the failure of the private sector to offer multiple-peril crop insurance have been put forward. Kramer (1983, 182), for example, pointed out that one reason for the large losses was drought but also suggested that a contributing factor in some cases was that private companies operated in geographic areas that were too small to permit risk spreading. Perhaps more fundamental problems, however, were those of adverse selection and moral hazard. Specific-peril crop insurance for hail and fire had been, and continues to be, offered successfully by private insurance companies. The occurrence of such specific perils is as easily identified by the insurer as by the insured farmer, and potential losses are also fairly easy to assess on a farm-by-farm basis. Thus, the scope for either moral hazard or adverse selection is limited. Monitoring and measuring costs for all-risk contracts, under which indemnities are paid if yields are low for (almost) any reason, are much higher and may well preclude such insurance contracts from being commercially viable. Regardless of the reasons, however, in the early 1920s the private sector did not offer such all-risk crop insurance contracts.

Congressional attention was drawn to the issue of crop losses in 1922 when the U.S. Department of Agriculture published information on crop damage from different causes such as drought, diseases, insects and other pests, and frost (Kramer 1983, 182). Subsequently, in 1923, congressional select committee hearings were held under the direction of Senators McNary (Oregon), Keyes (New Hampshire), and Smith (South Carolina). While at that time neither that select committee nor the Secretary of Agriculture Henry Wallace formally recommended that government enter the crop insurance market to provide all-risk crop insurance, Senator McNary later pushed strongly for the creation of a bureau within USDA to examine crop insurance (Kramer, 184).[2] In the late 1920s, however, agricultural policy debates began to focus on other innovations such as the McNary-Haugen two-price system proposal and Professor Black's proposed domestic allotment program that were the precursors of the provisions of the 1933 Agricultural Adjustment Act.

Interest in providing farmers with protection against low yields enjoyed a resurgence in 1936 after widespread droughts in 1934 and 1936 caused severe hardship within the farm sector and, in part, precipitated high rates of farm foreclosures and bankruptcies. At the 1936 Democratic convention in June, Henry Wallace campaigned un-

2. In the 1930s, Wallace also clearly changed his position and explicitly incorporated crop insurance as a component of his "ever normal granary" initiative.

successfully to include crop insurance as a part of the Democratic Platform (Kramer 1983, 185). Three months later, however, in September, six weeks before the presidential election, President Roosevelt's Republican opponent, Alf Landon, planned to give a speech in Des Moines, Iowa, in which he intended to declare that "the question of crop insurance should be given the fullest attention." Clearly, Landon hoped to garner votes from the agricultural sector, then a much larger constituency than it is now.[3] Two days before Landon was to give the speech, and probably with prior knowledge of its contents (Kramer 1983, 184), President Roosevelt appointed an interagency committee to examine the feasibility of government-sponsored crop insurance (Kramer 1983, 185). In 1936, research on the viability of crop insurance was also initiated at USDA using data on wheat and cotton yields collected over the previous five years by the Agricultural Adjustment Administration. Perhaps not surprisingly, USDA analysts concluded that data on wheat yields could provide an actuarial basis for crop insurance.

Roosevelt's interagency committee, which published its findings in 1937, recommended that a crop insurance program be established but, initially, only for wheat. Farmers would be insured against risks to their yield, but no protection against price variability would be offered. Public criticisms of the interagency committee's proposals were not lacking. The *Washington Post*, the *Christian Science Monitor*, and *Barron's*, then extremely politically influential publications,[4] were skeptical of such a program and, as Kramer points out, the *Christian Science Monitor's* editors were particularly astute in raising issues about

3. Over 20 percent of all households derived income from farming at that time.

4. The influence of these publications in forming and articulating informed public opinion was probably much more extensive than it is today because of lack of competition from television.

the federal crop insurance program that are as pertinent now as they were then when the editors asked:

> Will the program become in effect an underwriting of high-risk farming areas which in fact ought to be retired from farming and put to grazing, forests or other uses instead of burdening steadier farms with cutthroat competition in good years and a demand on them for assistance in bad years? (Kramer 1983, 186)

Barron's editors simply claimed that no actuarially sound crop insurance program could be "self-sustaining"—that is, in the absence of subsidies, almost no farmer would be willing to purchase such insurance—and urged Roosevelt "not to permit so-called crop insurance to conceal a subsidy to the politically important agricultural industry"[5] (Kramer 1983, 185). These criticisms fell on politically deaf ears. With the endorsement of leaders of large national farm organizations such as the Grange and the American Farm Bureau Federation, and the full support of President Roosevelt, an individual-yield, multiple-crop insurance program was included under Title V of the 1938 Agricultural Adjustment Act.

It seems clear, then, that an important midwife at the birth of the federal government crop insurance program was political expediency. Severe crop losses were engendered by both the 1934 and the 1936 droughts, but no policy initiative to deal with the hardships such events might impose on individual farmers was seriously considered until the 1936 election campaign. To the extent that economic welfare issues were raised with respect to

---

5. Evidence presented by Bardsley et al. (1984), as well as the pitiful record of private all-risk crop insurance initiatives and the consistent record of net losses associated with the USDA federal multiple-peril crop insurance program, tends to confirm that *Barron's* editors were right.

any justification for the program, income distribution concerns were dominant. President Roosevelt, formally and in writing, argued that crop insurance was needed for "alleviation of distress in rural areas arising out of factors beyond the control of individual producers" (Kramer 1983, 187). Apparently, no claim was made that a technical market failure deriving from externalities of one kind or another was preventing private markets from offering all-risk multiple-peril crop insurance at prices farmers were willing to pay.

In 1936, there certainly was good reason for policy makers to be concerned about the effects of low farm incomes on the economic status of many farm households. Before the 1940s, the money incomes of farm households were less than half those of urban dwellers (Pasour 1990), and many farm households also had few assets. When farm incomes fell sharply because of crop losses, as they did in 1934 and 1936, many of those households found themselves well over the wrong side of the poverty line.[6] Thus, government intervention to protect many farmers against crop losses caused by events beyond their control could have been justified on humanitarian grounds. Such considerations, though, are much less relevant today. Money incomes of farm households are roughly comparable with those of nonfarm households, and the average net worth of a farm household is about $700,000, as compared to about $75,000 for nonfarm households.

The History of the Federal Crop Insurance Program

The history of federal multiple-peril crop insurance between 1938 and 1994 can be usefully divided into four periods: 1938–1944, 1945–1973, 1973–1980, and 1981–1994. During the first period, 1938–1944, the program was established and operated for a limited range of commodi-

---

6. This was the era of American farm life described by John Steinbeck in *The Grapes of Wrath*.

ties. In 1944, after large subsidies were required to cover net losses, the program was discontinued for the 1944 crop year but, in response to political pressure, was reintroduced in 1945. During the second period, 1945–1973, the program was expanded to cover additional crops, although in 1947 sufficiently severe restrictions were placed on the scope of FCIC operations to lead commenters to describe the entire program, as it existed between 1947 and 1980, as experimental (Kramer 1983, 192). In 1973, the Agricultural and Consumer Protection Act established a mandatory federal disaster relief program, and during the third period, from 1973 to 1981, this new program operated in tandem and, in many counties, overlapped with the federal insurance program. The mandatory federal disaster program was discontinued at the beginning of 1981 after passage of the 1980 Federal Crop Insurance Act. As a result of this act, during the fourth period, 1981–1994, federal crop insurance became the only *before the fact* permanent disaster relief program for farmers. To function in this new role, the program was expanded to cover many more commodities in many more regions of the country.[7] Farmers in many states, however, did receive *after the fact* protection against crop loss through ad hoc emergency disaster relief legislation.

Throughout the fifty-six-year history of the federal crop insurance program, congressional concerns have focused on three major program-related issues: (1) net losses (or loss ratios) of the crop insurance program and the joint budgetary costs of the crop insurance and disaster relief programs; (2) the extent to which farms participate in the crop insurance program (that is, participation

---

7. The 1981, 1985, and 1990 farm bills all stipulated that disaster assistance would be made available for producers of program crops and, in addition, peanuts and soybeans in counties for which federal crop insurance was unavailable. This provided the FCIC with strong incentives to provide coverage for counties in which these crops were grown.

TABLE 3–1

ANNUAL AVERAGE TOTAL PREMIUMS, INDEMNITIES, AND LOSS
RATIOS FOR THE MPCI PROGRAM, 1939–1993

Period	Annual Average Premiums (millions of $)	Annual Average Indemnities (millions of $)	Annual Average Loss Ratios[a] (LR)	Number of years in which LR > 1
1939–43	58	97	1.65	4
1945–46	44	86	1.16	2
1947–55	195	226	1.16	5
1956–73	593	512	0.86	6
1976–80	674	888	1.32	4
1981–83	1245	1504	1.21	2
1984–90	4395	5766	1.32	7
1991–93	2251	3520	1.56	3

NOTE: After 1980, a 30 percent subsidy was built into the rate-setting
procedures.
a. This loss ratio is calculated as total indemnities divided by total premiums (including premium subsidies) and also does not
account for additional subsidies that covered FCIC's administrative expenses.
SOURCE: Federal Crop Insurance Corporation.

rates); and (3) in the 1980s and 1990s, arrangements for
marketing and servicing farmers' crop insurance contracts. From the perspective of successive administrations
and Congress, an ideal crop insurance program would
enjoy high participation rates and provide most farmers
with protection against yield losses but on average would
require no subsidies and would at the same time be available to all farms in all states and counties. The historical
evidence presented below suggests that, for individual
farm yield insurance based on voluntary participation,
these are mutually exclusive goals.

At the outset, it is useful to keep in mind an important aspect of the political economy of the crop insurance

program. Throughout its history, periods of relatively high loss ratios have been followed by substantial changes in the crop insurance program. Data on annual averages for total premiums, total indemnities, and loss ratios over the periods 1939–1943, 1945–1955, 1956–1973, 1976–1980, 1981–1983, 1984–1990, and 1991–1993 are presented in table 3–1. The periods are selected carefully to illustrate the effects and causes of important shifts in policy regimes. In all but one of these periods (1956–1973), loss ratios were greater than 1, and over the entire fifty-four-year period the average loss ratio has been 1.33.[8]

Period 1, 1938–1944. From 1939, the first year in which contracts were offered, to 1943, when the program was discontinued, farm premiums failed to cover losses in each year, the average loss ratio over the five-year period was 1.65 (for every dollar of premiums it received, the FCIC paid out $1.65), and annual subsidies (ignoring administrative overhead charges) averaged $11.7 million. There were good reasons for the actuarial problems the program encountered in its first year. First, local committees of the Agricultural Adjustment Administration were given the responsibility for administering the program at the farm level. This amounted to asking farmers to set premiums and assess losses for their neighbors, a situation fraught with the potential for moral-hazard problems. Second, very few farms provided sufficient data on yields for the committees to estimate expected individual farm losses. Lack of adequate data, therefore, resulted in rates for individual farms being established on the basis of countywide yield data, which exhibit much less variabil-

---

8. This figure may misstate the average loss ratio for the program in real terms over its history because, in computing the average loss ratio, no account has been taken of the effects of inflation on the purchasing power of the dollar and during earlier periods loss ratios were lower than during later periods.

ity than farm-level data. Inevitably, this approach caused expected losses to be underestimated and premium rates to be set too low. Third, through administrative delays many farmers were asked to sign contracts well after they had planted their crops. As a result, farmers with prospects of good crops let their contracts lapse, creating an extremely adversely selected pool of insured farmers. Some adjustments were made in premium rate-setting procedures in 1940 but produced no improvements in contract performance: loss ratios remained over 1.5 in both 1940 and 1941. In 1942, a cotton contract was introduced, but this contract also proved to be an actuarial disaster in both 1942 and 1943 (Kramer 1983). Thus, in 1943, Congress canceled the entire program because of high losses and, to add insult to injury, low participation rates (Botts 1943).

Period 2, 1944-1973. The apparent demise of the program turned out to be merely a one-year hiatus. The program was reestablished in the 1945 crop year for wheat, cotton, and flax. For the first time, Congress also authorized experimental insurance programs aimed at expanded participation across crops and the limitation of losses. Experimental programs, to be offered in no more than twenty counties and for no more than three years, were authorized for major crops such as corn, oats, barley, rye, tobacco, rice, peanuts, forest products, citrus fruits, and "any other agricultural commodity, if sufficient actuarial data are available" (Kramer 1983, 191). Despite several initiatives for reducing adverse-selection and moral-hazard problems (such as a progressive protection plan under which higher payments were made if crops were damaged later in the growing season and a three-year contract for wheat), the average loss ratio over the two-year period 1945–1946 of 1.95 was excessively high, and annual average premium subsidies amounted to $21 million.

A major reason for what were then regarded as large subsidies was the shift in 1946 to the exclusive use of county data to determine yield variability and premium rates (Kramer 1983, 193). A second reason may have been that crop insurance was offered in areas in which crop production was a marginal activity. Congress responded rapidly to the problems by passing amendments in 1947 that restricted the availability of crop insurance geographically for each crop, a practice that continued until 1980.[9] Between 1947 and 1955, the annual average loss ratio of 1.16 and the average annual premium subsidy of $3.4 million were both substantially lower than in previous years. Nevertheless, adverse selection was clearly a problem, and in 1955, the FCIC identified fourteen counties in Colorado, New Mexico, and Texas that would no longer be eligible for crop insurance. The FCIC estimated that if these fourteen counties had been excluded from the program over the period 1949–1954, premiums would have exceeded losses in all, instead of just two, of those six years (Kramer 1983, 195). These counties were also, of course, exactly the sort of areas that the editors of the *Christian Science Monitor* had in mind when, in 1936, they warned against the dangers of a crop insurance program encouraging production in marginal lands.

Between 1956 and 1973, the FCIC had two major concerns. First, the corporation was interested in increasing participation by extending the number of crops for which coverage would be available and increasing the number of counties within which farmers could purchase coverage for a specific crop. Second, for the most part, the FCIC wanted to avoid high loss ratios. Until 1967, the corporation enjoyed some success in these goals. Innovations were made with respect to crop coverage, but protection for new crops was usually offered in only a few counties.[10] During that period, loss ratios were smaller

9. In 1948, for example, wheat crop insurance was available in only 200 counties.

10. Kramer notes, for example, that peanut contracts were introduced in 1962 but only for farmers in four counties.

than 0.9 in eight of the eleven years. Participation was relatively modest, however. Thus, beginning in 1965, the FCIC extended the availability of crop insurance and reduced premium rates, which fell from an average of 6.9 percent of total liabilities between 1956 and 1963 to an average of 5.8 percent between 1964 and 1969 (Kramer 1983, 196). Not surprisingly, farmer participation increased, as did indemnities, which exceeded premiums in 1967, 1968, and 1969. With the advent of the Nixon administration, new managers were brought in to run the FCIC. In 1970, after an extensive review of the FCIC's programs, some high-loss crop insurance programs (for example, for potatoes) were canceled, and other programs were modified to reduce losses. As a result, in 1971 the loss ratio fell to 0.6 and stayed at that level until the 1974 crop year.

Period 3, 1973–1980. Institutionally, the period 1973–1980 was distinguished from the previous period only in that, during that time, a mandatory disaster payments program operated in tandem with the federal crop insurance program. The disaster program was authorized under the provisions of the 1974 farm bill (the Agricultural and Consumer Protection Act) and renewed under the 1977 farm bill (the Food and Agriculture Act). The crop insurance program operated by the FCIC changed very little over this period. Although the annual average loss ratio increased to 1.32, loss ratios exhibited considerable year-to-year variability, ranging from 0.5 in 1978 to 3.29 in 1980. Offerings did not expand to any measurable degree either with respect to the number of crops for which insurance contracts were offered or with respect to geography.[11]

---

11. In 1974, federal crop insurance contracts were offered for at least one crop in 1,432 counties. In 1980, such contracts were offered in 1,676 counties, an increase of only 15.6 percent over the seven-year period. In contrast, as a result of reforms intro-

Year-to-year changes in loss ratios were largely the result of changes in growing conditions. In 1974, for example, growing conditions were particularly adverse in some regions for wheat and corn and, in 1980, for soybeans, tobacco, and other crops. Subsidies of indemnities during this period totaled $214 million (about $40 million per year) but represented a much smaller share of the federal budget than the losses incurred in the early 1940s. Major changes, however, were made to the federal crop insurance program in 1981 through the provisions of the 1980 Federal Crop Insurance Act.

The radical revisions to the federal crop insurance program made in 1980 were, for once, not driven directly by concerns about federal crop insurance losses and loss ratios but by concerns about the costs of the mandatory disaster relief program introduced in 1973. Between 1974 and 1980, disaster payments made under this program amounted to $3.39 billion, about eight times as much as the subsidies required for the crop insurance program over the same period. Kramer has noted that the mandatory disaster program was subject to the following three major criticisms:

- It encouraged production in high-risk areas (Gardner 1979).
- It insured against moral-hazard actions.
- It encouraged adverse selection by encouraging farmers to accept indemnities rather than plant under marginal growing conditions.

The quantitative effects of each of these factors on the program's costs have not been estimated. It was clear, however, to Congress and the Carter administration that

duced in 1980, by 1982 the number of counties in which insurance contracts were available for at least one crop had almost doubled to 2,999 counties.

the program was expensive and a potential political liability. A 1977 General Accounting Office (GAO) report had pointed out that a program in which farmers paid at least something for protection against yield disasters was likely to be less costly to the taxpayer than a program under which they paid nothing. In addition, the GAO report argued that the availability of free protection against large yield losses through the disaster program was likely to have undercut participation in the less actuarially unsound but, to the farmer, more costly federal crop insurance program. Thus, in 1977, Congress asked the secretary of agriculture to study alternative programs to provide "an all-risk, all-crop insurance to help provide protection to those suffering crop losses in floods, drought and other natural disasters." The Carter administration received recommendations from the secretary of agriculture in 1978 and requested that Congress act on them in 1978. Two years later, Congress passed the 1980 Federal Crop Insurance Act.

Period 4, 1981–1994. The 1980 Federal Crop Insurance Act introduced radical changes to the federal crop insurance program. The explicit intent of the act was to expand the program to ensure that most farmers in all geographic regions of the country would be able to purchase crop insurance against losses for all crops. The act therefore established a target goal of 50 percent participation in the program.[12] With this goal in mind, the following major changes were made in the program.

First, farms would be able to choose three levels of insurance coverage relative to their average yields (50 percent, 65 percent, and 75 percent), and the government would subsidize 30 percent of the premium cost to the

12. The definition of participation used by the FCIC is the percentage of planted acres eligible for insurance that is actually insured.

farmer for up to 65 percent coverage. If the farmer chose to buy 75 percent coverage, premiums would have to be set so that the additional coverage would be actuarially sound (that is, the additional premiums would have to cover the additional expected losses from the expanded coverage). The intent and the effect of the subsidy were unambiguously to make crop insurance more attractive to farmers.

Second, all annual restrictions on expansion of the program were removed. The purpose of the 1980 act was to develop a program under which the nationwide disaster relief program would be rapidly replaced by an almost universal federal crop insurance program. The restrictions on growth in place since 1947, while almost certainly successful as a means of constraining loss ratios and limiting taxpayer subsidies, were incompatible with this objective. Under the 1980 act, therefore, the FCIC was given a broad mandate to develop insurance contracts for new crops in existing counties and existing crops in new counties.

Third, major changes were introduced in the crop insurance marketing system. Before 1981, under provisions introduced in 1947, private companies could sell crop insurance contracts and be reinsured for their losses by the federal government. For each crop, however, the maximum number of counties in which these private reinsurance companies could market and service these contracts was very limited. Since 1981, private reinsurance companies have been permitted to sell multiple-peril crop insurance contracts for all crops in all counties for which contracts have been approved. Over the period 1981–1994, as is shown below, this innovation has radically altered the way in which multiple-peril crop insurance contracts have been marketed and serviced.

The first two changes in legislation under which the FCIC operated were clearly intended to increase partici-

TABLE 3–2
PARTICIPATION RATES FOR MPCI FOR ALL CROPS, 1980–1992
(percent)

Year	Participation Rates[a]
1980	10
1981	16
1982	15
1983	12
1984	16[b]
1985	18
1986	20
1987	20
1988	23
1989	40[c]
1990	40
1991	33
1992	32

a. The participation rate is defined as acreage insured under MPCI contracts divided by the potentially insurable acres (the total acreage that could have been covered).
b. After 1983, farms could insure separate tracts or units under separate contracts.
c. In 1989 and 1990, farmers who received emergency disaster relief payments in the previous year were required to purchase MPCI to be eligible for other government program benefits.
SOURCE: Federal Crop Insurance Corporation.

pation in the program. As the data on participation rates in the 1980s presented in table 3–2 show, however, the incentives provided by the premium subsidies were not sufficient to generate participation rates above 50 percent.[13] One reason for low participation rates for 1981–1994 was the implicit deductible built into the contracts. Un-

13. Although in 1989 the participation rate was about 40 percent, this was only because farmers receiving ad hoc disaster payments in 1988 (the third-worst drought year of the century) were required to purchase multiple-peril crop insurance in 1989 if they wanted to participate in major federal commodity programs and receive deficiency payments and other benefits from those programs.

der the contract providing maximum coverage, a farmer's crop yield had to fall below 75 percent of the average yield allocated to the farm. Many farmers almost never experience yields that fall more than 25 percent below their average yields.[14] A second reason has been the problem of adverse selection. Until 1982, premium rates for individual farms were set on a countywide basis, using countywide information on variability of yields and average yields. Premium rates, therefore, tended to reflect expected losses for the average farm within a county. Some farms, however, experienced much less variability (and therefore had much lower expected losses) than other farms. For such farms, premium rates were simply set too high.

This adverse-selection problem was widely recognized, and in 1983 a new rate-setting procedure based on an individual farm's actual production history was introduced. Under that rate-setting procedure, farmers who could provide ten years of yield history would be charged premiums based on that yield history. Individual yield histories, however, were to be used only to establish the farm's average yield for each crop.[15] Information on the variability of the yield of an individual farm was generally ignored, and farms within a given county were charged identical premium rates, regardless of any evidence about individual yield variability and expected losses.[16]

---

14. This is especially true for irrigated crops. Zering et al. (1987), in a study of thirty-two irrigated cotton and soybean operations in California, reported that only one or two farms ever expected to experience such low yields (in the absence of earthquakes or other large-scale disasters that would almost certainly trigger ad hoc disaster relief aid).

15. In addition, farmers that experienced very low yields in one or more years could quite easily have at least one such year replaced by the county average yield (and probably more than just one year). Thus penalties for experiencing low yields and receiving frequent indemnities were very mild.

16. Exceptions were made in the case of a few farms that, almost pathologically, were able to collect indemnities in almost every year.

TABLE 3–3

GEOGRAPHIC AND CROP COVERAGE OFFERED UNDER THE MPCI
PROGRAM, 1980–1993

Year	Total Number of Crops Covered	Number of Counties with at Least One Crop Program	Total Number of County Crop Programs[a]
1980	28	1,676	4,651
1981	29	1,928	5,944
1982	30	2,999	14,588
1983	30	3,000	15,415
1984	34	3,010	17,879
1985	38	3,012	18,903
1986	40	3,013	19,064
1987	44	3,014	19,263
1988	44	3,015	19,675
1989	49	3,022	20,507
1990	50	3,026	23,533
1991	51	3,026	24,399
1992	51	3,026	24,414
1993	51	3,026	24,587

a. The total number of county crop programs is the sum of all individual crop programs offered in each county.
SOURCE: Federal Crop Insurance Corporation.

This approach received some validation from an analysis by Skees and Reed (1986) of the relationship between average yields and measures of yield variability for corn and soybean producers in Kentucky. Skees and Reed reported that as average farm yields rose, variability (measured by the standard deviation of yields) did not, and therefore suggested that premium rates set according to the farm's average yield would largely solve the adverse-selection problem. Their findings, however, have not been confirmed by other studies (for example, Goodwin and Kastens 1993; Goodwin 1993; Just and Calvin 1990; Smith and Baquet 1993). What is more, Goodwin (1994) and Goodwin and Kerr (1994) have recently shown that relying on mean yields as a means of setting premium rates does not solve the adverse-selection problem even if there is no general statistical relationship between average yields and yield variability. In that case, two farms with the same average yields are likely to have very different yield distributions and differ markedly with respect to the indemnities they expect to receive from the same crop insurance contract.

Certainly, in the 1980s the scope of the crop insurance program did increase rapidly. Table 3–3 presents data on the number of counties in which at least one crop is covered by federal crop insurance contracts, the number of crops for which crop insurance contracts are available, and the total number of county programs offered.[17] As a result of relaxing restrictions on the expansion of existing crop programs into new counties and the development of programs for new crops, the number of counties in which some crop insurance was offered jumped from 1,656 in 1980 to 2,999 in 1983. Most of this expansion, however, occurred because the FCIC increased the number of counties in which insurance contracts for major crops such as wheat, corn, and soybeans were available. During these two years, new insurance contracts were developed for only two new crops.[18] After 1983, most of the expansion took the form of the provisions of contracts for new crops in counties in which crop insurance was already available for other crops. Between 1983 and 1991, crop insurance programs were introduced into only fifteen new counties, but contracts were developed for twenty new crops.

Participation rates, measured by the ratio of insured acres to total acres for which insurance could have been purchased, did not increase very much, although there

17. This is equal to the sum, across crops, of the number of counties in which a given crop is covered by crop insurance.

18. This is not surprising. It takes two or three years for the FCIC to develop any actuarial basis for insurance contracts for new crops.

was a jump in the participation rate after 1983. This increase might be attributable to the introduction of new rate-setting procedures that also took place in 1983. Another often overlooked, but extremely important innovation in the program, however, also took place in 1983. Until 1983, wheat and other grains producers were required to insure all the acreage for a specific crop under the same contract. After 1983, under what is known as the units provision, farmers could insure each tract of land planted to a specific crop under a separate contract. This benefited large farms (for example, grain-producing farms in Texas and the Great Plains that typically cover several thousand acres) that often have better yields on one tract than on another tract. Before 1984, given the requirement that all acreage for a specific crop be insured under the same contract, such farms were much less likely to receive indemnities than afterward, even if average yields on each tract were approximately identical. Certainly, as the data in table 3–1 show, the aggregate loss ratio for the program rose from an annual average of 1.21 between 1981 and 1983 to an annual average of 1.32 between 1984 and 1990. This increase was partly driven by the geographic expansion of the program, partly caused by severe droughts in 1985 and 1988, but was also partly a result of the 1983 innovation that allowed farms to partition acreage for insurance purposes.

Changes in the marketing and servicing of federal crop insurance contracts were also blamed for some of the increase in loss ratios that occurred during the 1980s. We have already noted that the 1980 act introduced legislative changes that radically altered the way in which these contracts were marketed and serviced. Before 1981, contracts were also sold and serviced primarily by FCIC employees, usually on a part-time basis. Some contracts were sold by staff in ASCS county offices and a small number of independent agents operating under a sales and service agreement (GAO 1983). Loss assessments for all contracts were carried out by FCIC staff or, on an experimental basis, by private loss adjusters hired and monitored by the FCIC. The 1980 act introduced two new arrangements for the sale and servicing of crop insurance contracts, both of which relied on the private sector for the delivery of marketing services—master marketing sales contracts and private reinsurance contracts. In 1983, these mechanisms became the only marketing vehicles for federal crop insurance contracts, because by then, as a matter of policy, sales by ASCS and FCIC staff had been phased out.

Under a master marketing contract, an insurance agent agrees to sell MPCI contracts to individual farmers in return for a fixed percentage of the total premiums generated by those sales. The insurance agent's responsibilities end, however, once the farmer has signed the insurance contract; servicing the contract and adjusting losses then become the responsibility of FCIC employees. Under a reinsurance contract, an insurance company not only markets MPCI contracts but also services them and adjusts losses to determine indemnities. Reinsurance companies receive a much higher fraction of the premium paid by MPCI purchasers than do master marketers because the former sell and service MPCI contracts and act as loss adjusters. Reinsurance companies, however, can incur limited penalties on losses from their portfolios of crop insurance contracts. Throughout the period 1981–1992, these penalties were small (amounting to a maximum penalty of less than 10 percent of the income received by reinsurance companies for their services). In 1993, however, the penalties reinsurance companies incurred for losses increased quite substantially.

The dual role of reinsurance companies as marketers and loss appraisers has been controversial. Several GAO reports (see, for example, the GAO reports published in 1983, 1987, and 1989) were critical of the structure of reinsurance contracts and, in 1983, congressional

TABLE 3–4
SHARES OF MPCI MARKETING SALES BY TYPE OF SALES ORGANIZATION, 1983–1993

Year	Percentage of Sales by Master Marketers	Percentage of Sales by Private Reinsurance Companies
1983	63.6	36.4
1984	40.3	59.7
1985	26.1	73.9
1986	19.5	80.5
1987	16.0	84.0
1988	13.7	86.3
1989	9.6	90.4
1990	10.2	89.8
1991	9.7	90.3
1992	8.2	91.8
1993	6.8	93.2

SOURCE: Federal Crop Insurance Corporation.

hearings were held on the issue. The GAO reports emphasized that loss ratios were higher for reinsurance contracts than for master marketer contracts and pointed out that a moral-hazard problem existed with the reinsurance contract. Throughout the 1980s and early 1990s, under the standard reinsurance contract, reinsurance companies bore no penalties for indemnities associated with their portfolios until losses rose to more than 110 percent of total premiums. Then they were required to bear 2 percent of all additional losses up to a penalty cap of approximately 10 percent of their revenues from sales (which would occur when the loss ratio on a company's portfolio reached 5.4). These provisions meant that in most years reinsurance companies experienced no penalties from losses when they made loss adjustments. Thus, one low-cost tool available to reinsurance companies for obtaining new business and ensuring repeat business was to be generous in assessing losses. On several occasions, the GAO recommended that reinsurance companies be "asked" to bear a larger share of the risks of loss, but no serious response to these recommendations occurred until 1993, by which time, as is shown in table 3–1, the annual average loss ratio for the MPCI program had risen to well over 1.5.

In fact, over the period 1983–1993 private reinsurance companies gradually became the most important marketers of MPCI contracts. The data presented in table 3–4 show the annual percentages of total liabilities sold by master marketers and reinsurance companies over the period 1983–1993. At the beginning of this period, master marketers made about 50 percent of total sales; by 1993, their share of total sales had fallen to less than 10 percent. This shift was driven by FCIC policy under which returns to master marketers from each dollar of liabilities sold gradually declined, while returns to private reinsurance companies remained fairly stable. One reason for this policy was to reduce the need for government involvement in the servicing of MPCI contracts. The 1981–1993 Reagan and Bush administrations believed in moderating government involvement in activities that could be carried out by private companies. In this case, loss adjustment responsibilities were transferred to the private sector but ironically because (until 1993) reinsurance companies faced very little risk of loss, this strategy probably did not reduce total program costs, although it probably did result in a minimal reduction in the size of the government bureaucracy.

Between 1983 and 1990, the MPCI program experienced loss ratios well in excess of 1, and annual government subsidies to the program rose steadily. At the same time, as we show below, expensive ad hoc disaster relief legislation was regularly passed by Congress to compensate farmers in areas suffering from natural disasters for catastrophic losses. Thus, during the debate over the 1990 farm bill, the Bush administration identified federal crop insurance as a program to be abolished and replaced by an area-triggered standing disaster program. While in the end no major changes were made to the program in the 1990 Food, Agriculture, Conservation, and Trade Act, Congress did make provision for the FCIC to introduce new types of insurance contracts on an experimental basis and sent the FCIC a very clear message that its major concern should be to reduce loss ratios and the subsidy costs of its programs.

Until 1990, FCIC initiatives (through geographic expansion and the introduction of multiple-peril crop insurance contracts for new crops) had been aimed at increasing access to and participation in the MPCI program. From 1991 to 1994, the FCIC focused more intently on potential solutions to the problems of high loss ratios and high taxpayer costs. As a result, some important changes were made in the MPCI program. First, in 1993 a policy decision was made to increase premium rates substantially, and premium rates for the 1994 crop year were sharply increased by between 10 and 20 percent.[19] Second, the FCIC introduced substantial changes in the actual production history method by which a farm's average yield is computed. Under the revised method, introduced in 1994, if a farm cannot show at least four years of "proven" yield history, it is assigned a very low average yield for insurance purposes. The intent of this reform was to reduce problems of adverse selection. Penalties for fraud were also increased. Farmers who attempted to misrepresent their yield histories could now be denied all other farm program benefits for two years. Third, the FCIC instituted a "nonstandard classification system" that allowed the corporation to underwrite farms with "habitual" losses individually. The nonstandard classification approach resulted in substantially higher premiums for many soybean producers in the Mississippi Delta and the southeast, and losses on such contracts declined substantially.

19. Under the provisions of the 1980 FCIA, 20 percent is the maximum permitted year-to-year increase in premium rates for any crop.

Area-Yield Crop Insurance

Under the provisions of the 1990 Food, Agriculture, Conservation, and Trade Act, the FCIC was also given the authority to examine and, on an experimental or pilot basis, to implement other types of insurance contracts with some potential for reducing loss ratios and subsidies, while still offering farmers protection against risk of loss. The type of contract that has been given the most extensive consideration by the FCIC is an area-yield contract. Under area-yield contracts, farmers receive indemnities when the actual countywide per acre average yield falls below a prespecified proportion of the county's expected or long-run per acre average yield.

The idea of area-yield crop insurance is not new. In 1949, Halcrow proposed area-yield crop insurance as an alternative to individual-yield crop insurance to resolve problems of adverse selection and moral hazard. His proposal was largely ignored until 1991 when, in a widely cited paper in the *American Journal of Agricultural Economics*, Miranda examined the relative effects of area-yield and individual-yield contracts on the variance of net farm yields and (by implication) gross returns.[20] Miranda considered an area-yield contract that had two components, a critical area yield, y_c, which would trigger indemnity payments, and a coverage level, ϕ. When area yield, y, falls below the critical yield, assuming for simplicity that indemnities are paid in bushels per acre, indemnities received by the farmer, n, equal $\phi_i(y_{ci} - y)$; when y exceeds y_{ci} then n is zero. Under the Miranda contract, the farm makes two choices. First, it selects the critical yield, $y_{ci} = \alpha_i \mu$, by determining the proportion, α_i, of the long-run average or expected area yield, μ, against which it wants to insure, and then it selects its coverage level. Miranda

20. The idea of area-yield crop insurance contracts was introduced into contemporary debates over crop insurance returns by Barnaby and Skees in 1990.

showed that such a two-step "ideal" contract provided most farms with substantial reduction in net yield variations although less than under individual-yield contracts.

Area-yield contracts are widely believed to reduce incentives for moral-hazard behavior at the farm level. Typically, the individual farm's yields will have only a small impact on area yields and therefore area-yield crop insurance contracts do not provide incentives for moral hazard. Nor within a given county is there any incentive for adverse selection. As Goodwin has noted, however, adverse selection may well be a problem at the county level. There is no guarantee that the FCIC will set premiums correctly for all counties. Thus, in counties in which expected payoffs from the insurance contract are positive (that is, premiums are smaller than expected indemnities per dollar of liability), many farmers will sign up for area-yield coverage; in counties with negative payoffs (where premiums are larger than expected indemnities per dollar of liability), few farmers will sign up. Thus, on balance, errors in rate setting could still lead to problems of adverse selection for the program as a whole.

If, however, individual-yield contracts are inseparable from irreducible moral-hazard problems, then an area-yield program, which offers some protection against yield risk to most farmers but vastly reduces incentives for these problems, may be a viable alternative to an individual-yield program. In 1993, the FCIC introduced area-yield contracts for soybeans and wheat in more than 100 selected counties. In addition, in the spring of 1994, similar contracts were offered in more than 1,200 counties for barley, corn, cotton, peanuts, and grain sorghum. The pilot area-yield contracts, described as Group Risk Plans, were very similar to the one proposed by Miranda in that each farm could choose its trigger yield by picking an α_i and, in addition, select a coverage level, ϕ_i. One important difference was that under the pilot program the trigger yield could be no greater than 90 percent of the long-run average area (county) yield and the coverage level could be no greater than 150 percent; that is, $\alpha_i \leq 0.9$ and $\phi_i \leq 1.5$. The other was that indemnities were calculated slightly differently so that, as area yields fell by one bushel, indemnities rose by slightly more than one bushel.

The Group Risk Plan area-yield contracts have been largely ignored by farmers in counties in which such contracts were offered. Among Montana winter wheat producers, no farmer purchased a Group Risk Plan contract. Similar responses welcomed the advent of such contracts in other states. Nationwide, only 2,700 farmers purchased those contracts in 1994, although they were offered in over 1,200 counties (more than one-third of all counties in the nation). One reason for extremely low participation in the Group Risk Plan may simply have been lack of knowledge on the part of farmers (because of lack of experience within the farming community) about the potential benefits of the program. Smith et al. (1994), however, have shown that premiums for area-yield contracts that provide about the same amount of reduction in risk as actuarially identical multiple-peril crop insurance contracts have premium rates that are between two and five times larger than the premiums for the multiple-peril contracts. Farmers concerned about cash flows will therefore prefer multiple-peril contracts even if they are actuarially equivalent to area-yield contracts. Given that area-yield contracts, in contrast to multiple-peril contracts, offer farmers little or no opportunity to practice moral hazard, it is not surprising that the area-yield program has not passed its marketplace test. A second reason, as Gantz (1994) has recently noted, may have been opposition to the Group Risk Plan on the part of private insurance companies that perceived that those contracts provided them with lower reimbursement rates than MPCI contracts.

Federal Disaster Payment Programs

Emergency loans and government payments for disaster relief have been provided in various forms since the nineteenth century. Until recently, most of this assistance was given in the form of grants and loans to replace public facilities damaged by natural or man-made disasters. Congress formally established a continuing disaster aid program in 1949 through the Farmers Home Administration emergency disaster loan program. Under this program, farmers who experienced severe crop losses as a result of natural disasters were eligible for special low-interest loans.

Disaster payment programs were introduced in the early 1970s. The Agricultural and Consumer Protection Act of 1973 and the Rice Production Act of 1975 established disaster payment programs that covered wheat, upland cotton, and feedgrains. To be eligible for disaster payments, farmers had to have base acreage allotments and were thus required to participate in Commodity Credit Corporation farm programs. Payments were made for prevented plantings or underplantings that occurred because of drought, flood, or other natural conditions. Payments were also made for low yields, with payment levels based on the extent to which an individual's yield fell below established yields, which were calculated from county average yields. Yields that fell below 66.67 percent of the farm's established yield triggered disaster payments. Payment rates (dollars per bushel or shortfall) were set at one-third of the target prices established by the 1973 act. Payment limits of $20,000 per farmer were established.

In the 1974 crop year, adverse weather caused widespread yield shortfalls for covered crops. Under the 1974 program, 580,000 applications for disaster payments were submitted. Of these, 476,000 (from 321,500 farms) were approved. Disaster payments in fiscal year 1975 exceeded $555 million (ASCS). Of this amount, corn received 43.9 percent, upland cotton received 23.9 percent, and wheat received 18.2 percent. In fiscal years 1976 and 1977, payments exceeding $286 million and $82 million were paid to farmers (ASCS 1994).

The Food and Agriculture Act of 1977 renewed the

mandatory disaster payment program even though concerns had been raised about the budget cost of the program by both Congress and the Carter administration. Under the 1977 act, payments were triggered when wheat and feedgrain yields fell below 60 percent of normal and when cotton and rice yields fell below 75 percent of normal. The program ended in 1981. Between fiscal year 1975 and fiscal year 1981, CCC outlays for disaster payments exceeded $3.57 billion (ASCS 1994).

Outlays for disaster assistance eased between fiscal years 1982 and 1988. The FY 1987 omnibus spending bill allocated $400 million to cover drought and flood losses of farmers, mainly in the Southeast. The Farm Disaster Assistance Act of 1987 supplemented the 1986 assistance with $135 million for Midwestern farmers who were unable to plant winter wheat in the preceding fall because of flooding. Following widespread drought in 1988, Congress passed the Disaster Assistance Act of 1988. Disaster payments in fiscal year 1989 exceeded $4 billion, representing the largest nominal expenditure on disaster relief in history. In every year that followed with the exception of 1991, annual expenditures on disaster payments exceeded $1 billion. The Disaster Assistance Act of 1989 allocated $1.48 billion to cover drought losses. Title XXII of the 1990 Farm Bill authorized disaster payments for weather-related losses. The widespread flooding and drought of 1993 and 1994 brought forth the Midwest Flood and Southeast Drought Aid Act that provided $3.25 billion in agricultural disaster payments.

Before the 1994 Crop Insurance Reform Act, ASCS disaster relief provisions for uninsured farmers paid for shortfalls below 60 percent of the farms' ASCS yields at 65 percent of the relevant price. For many farmers who also purchased multiple-peril crop insurance, payments were triggered for yields below 65 percent of normal yields. For farmers in the commodity program who were producing program crops, the disaster price was the target price. For farmers not in the commodity program who

FIGURE 3–1
Disaster Payments and Insurance Indemnities in Nine States following the 1993 Midwestern Flood
(millions of dollars)

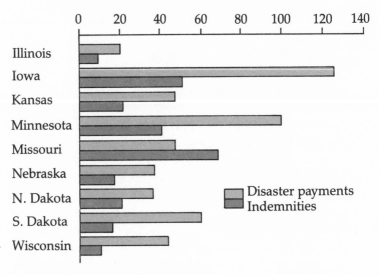

Source: Leppert and McIlwain 1994.

were producing program crops, disaster payments were based on the county loan rate. For nonprogram crops, payments were based on the five-year national market average price.

The 1993 Midwestern flood brought about significant crop losses as well as substantial losses by homeowners and nonagricultural businesses. ASCS-administered disaster payment programs dispensed over $3.1 billion in disaster relief in fiscal year 1994. Over $1.6 billion was spent on the nine Midwestern states directly affected by the 1993 flood (Illinois, Iowa, Kansas, Minnesota, Missouri, Nebraska, North Dakota, South Dakota, and Wisconsin).

As Gardner and Kramer (1986) noted, disaster payment programs are popular with farmers because they

FIGURE 3–2

NUMBERS OF PRODUCERS RECEIVING DISASTER PAYMENTS AND
INSURANCE INDEMNITIES IN NINE STATES FOLLOWING THE 1993
MIDWESTERN FLOOD

(thousands)

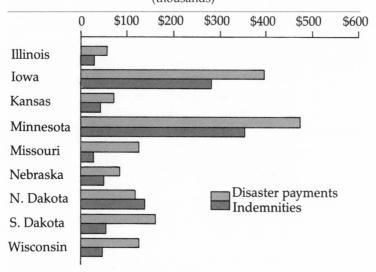

SOURCE: Leppert and McIlwain 1994.

provide farmers with free disaster protection with coverage in high-risk areas where crop insurance may not have
been available. Disaster relief programs have been criti-
cized, however, not only because of their high costs but
also because they are said to encourage production in
areas especially susceptible to natural disasters.

An examination of budget outlays on disaster payment programs and the federal crop insurance program
that occurred because of the 1993 flood reveals many of
the concerns about the interaction of disaster relief and
crop insurance programs. Figure 3-1 illustrates disaster
payments and crop insurance indemnities for the nine
Midwestern states affected by the flood. In every state
except North Dakota, disaster payments exceeded crop
insurance indemnities. Figure 3-2 shows the frequency

of disaster payments and indemnities following the 1993 flood. In every state, the number of producers receiving disaster payments significantly exceeds the number of producers receiving crop insurance indemnities. This finding confirms that many producers who did not purchase crop insurance were reimbursed for their losses under the disaster payment program. This further demonstrates the "free insurance" nature of disaster relief programs. Participation in the federal crop insurance program is much lower than participation in ad hoc disaster relief programs in periods following natural disasters, and many producers who did not buy insurance are nonetheless compensated by the federal government for their losses.

Conclusions

The historical evidence presented in this chapter indicates that, as for many other government policies, changes in U.S. crop insurance and disaster programs have been driven by concerns about their benefits and budgetary costs. Standard political economy issues have played a major role in this regard. The crop insurance program came into existence in large part because it was a vote winner among an important rural constituency in the 1936 presidential election. Similarly, the original 1973 disaster program and subsequent ad hoc disaster relief bills were perceived to provide political capital for congressional delegates and presidents during the mid- and late 1980s. When these programs resulted in large costs for the Treasury (as was the case for the crop insurance program in the early 1940s, the early 1950s, and the early 1990s and for the mandatory and ad hoc disaster relief programs in the late 1970s and early 1990s), changes in those programs designed to reduce such costs soon followed.

Ironically, however, very little attempt has been made to justify these programs on the grounds that some market failure exists in the insurance industry. Arguments for programs that enhanced farm incomes during "disaster" years when crop yields were low were used to buttress the case for a crop insurance program in the mid-1930s, a period when the cash incomes of farm households were low relative to the cash incomes of nonfarm households. Such is not the case today, however. It seems reasonable, then, to conclude that the forces that created and sustained disaster programs in the United States resulted from rent-seeking activities on the part of interest groups and concerns about political support on the part of policy makers. Understanding why market failures have not been viewed as important issues in debates over disaster assistance and crop insurance programs requires an appreciation of the economic forces that determine the behavior of insurance markets. In the next chapter, therefore, these issues are addressed through a theoretical discussion of the economics of insurance markets.

4
The Theory of Disaster Relief and Insurance

A private market for crop insurance will exist when farmers are willing to purchase crop insurance contracts at a price at which insurers are willing to sell such contracts. This chapter examines the willingness of individuals to pay for protection against risk and the implications of such willingness to pay for the demand for insurance. Sources of adverse-selection and moral-hazard problems, which have significant implications for the structure and viability of crop insurance markets, are then examined. Next, the conditions under which insurers would be willing to offer insurance contracts are investigated, and the implications of moral-hazard problems for the viability of private insurance markets are identified. Finally, we consider whether there is any reason to believe that private multiple-peril crop insurance markets have been unsuccessful because of technical market failures. No compelling evidence for such market failures seems to exist. First, however, we discuss the effects of free disaster relief programs (for which income distribution and equity concerns or political economy considerations are the only theoretical rationales) on participation in only partially subsidized multiple-peril crop insurance programs.

Disaster Relief Programs

One of the most serious factors thought to inhibit participation in the federal crop insurance program is the ad
hoc provision of disaster relief programs.[1] During the
1980s, over $19 billion was spent on direct disaster relief
programs. This figure represented 76 percent of total outlays realized by the USDA for insurance and disaster-re-
lated programs. The recurring nature of disaster payment
programs suggests that producers may have come to expect disaster payments during periods of catastrophic
yield losses. In this light, disaster relief programs are
analogous to free catastrophic insurance, which would
be expected to pay "indemnities" in the event of widespread losses.

The expectation of ad hoc disaster relief measures
during periods of severe yield shortfalls is likely to be
especially discouraging to the insurance purchases of low-
risk producers. Disaster relief measures occur most often
when yield losses are widespread. When disaster relief
measures are likely in the event of widespread losses, low-
risk individuals typically realize that, if they suffer losses,
losses are likely to be widespread and thus that disaster
relief measures will likely be forthcoming. Recent experiences with the droughts of 1988, 1989, and 1993 and extensive flooding in 1993 and 1994 confirm the likelihood
of ad hoc government disaster relief. In such an environment, low-risk individuals have a diminished incentive
to purchase insurance. Thus, disaster relief measures may
not only reduce participation but also have the second-
ary impact of increasing the riskiness of the insurance pool.

By their very nature, disaster relief programs are ad
hoc. That is, such programs are not planned and are thus

1. This point is not specific to crop insurance. A recent Interagency Flood Plain Management Review Committee report
(1994) concluded that disaster relief provisions greatly limited
purchases of federal flood insurance.

not part of standard budget debates and constraints. In this context, expenditures on ad hoc disaster relief programs are not disciplined in the same way as other budgetary policy items. Disaster relief programs are not budgetary line items in the presidential budget. Further, the provision of such relief may be sensitive to political pressures and inequities in political influence.

In a theoretical context, disaster relief can be thought of in the same political economy terms as other measures of agricultural support, that is, as income transfers from taxpayers to farmers. Representatives from areas that suffer serious yield shortfalls have political incentives to secure support for their district or state. Disasters are usually geographically localized but widespread within the affected location. Thus, individual politicians have strong incentives to work for transfers from the national treasury to alleviate disasters in their home constituencies.

Assumptions Underlying the Theory of Insurance

The theory of insurance has its underpinnings in the neoclassical theory of behavior under uncertainty. Laffont (1989) states that that theory essentially describes the implications of rational choice under conditions of uncertainty. In this context, agents are usually assumed to maximize their expected utility. In their classic development of the theory of games, von Neumann and Morgenstern (1944) articulated the theory that underlies the expected utility hypothesis. Von Neumann and Morgenstern's expected utility theory forms the basis for most theoretical considerations of the demand for insurance. The theory assumes perfect information in that the probabilities governing alternative outcomes are assumed to be known with certainty. A distinction between risk and uncertainty is sometimes made in regard to this issue. Using Knight's (1965) terminology, risk refers to situations for which the probabilities of various outcomes are known completely by agents. Conversely, uncertainty implies that the probabilities are unknown. Most theoretical considerations of the demand for insurance assume that outcomes are risky but that the probabilities governing these outcomes are known to agents.

Under the axioms developed by Von Neumann and Morgenstern (1944), an agent facing s possible outcomes will act to maximize expected utility, which is given by:

$$\Sigma_{s=1}^{S} \; \pi_s u(x_s), \tag{4-1}$$

where π_s represents the probability of the sth outcome, x_s represents the expected value of the sth outcome, and u( ) is a utility function. Thus, agents maximize a weighted-average type utility function where the weights are given by probabilities of alternative event outcomes.

The Risk-Aversion Paradigm

The neoclassical theory of producer choice under uncertainty almost universally assumes that agents are globally averse to risk. This assumption, in turn, implies that rational agents will always be willing to pay some positive amount to lower risk, holding expected returns constant. Determining the proper representation of risk preferences and empirically measuring those preferences are difficult. Agents' risk preferences often vary according to the situation, context, and magnitude of the problem. Agents' reactions to small losses, for example, may differ from their reaction to small gains occurring with equal probabilities in ways not consistent with the expected utility hypothesis.[2] Another complication arises from the fact that most economic variables important to agents' expected

---

2. Many of the inconsistencies in the expected utility hypothesis and the risk-aversion paradigm are evaluated by Kahneman and Tversky (1979). Their analysis presents an alternative view of risk preferences (prospect theory), which allows preferences to vary according to the situation and context.

utility maximization problems are random. The probability distributions of various factors may not be independent. Yield and price, for example, are likely to be inversely correlated. This relationship may complicate the representation and measurement of event probabilities.

Insurance models implicitly adhere to the risk-aversion paradigm: all agents are risk averse and are thus willing to insure at actuarially fair premium rates (a result demonstrated below). As was noted in chapter 3, however, premium rates in the federal crop insurance program are not actuarially fair. During the 1980s, the average farmer received $1.88 in indemnities for every dollar paid in premiums (U.S. General Accounting Office 1983, 1987, 1989). The federal crop insurance program therefore provides positive expected returns for many participants, and thus the question of whether risk aversion is a necessary (or relevant) assumption becomes germane. Agents with a preference for risk could choose to purchase insurance in the case of contracts with positive expected returns. In this case, distortions in premiums caused by adverse selection may be more relevant to insurance purchase decisions than risk preferences.

The Theory of the Demand for Insurance

The theoretical foundations of the demand for insurance and for the design of insurance contracts were developed by Borch (1962, 1989), Arrow (1963), Rothschild and Stiglitz (1977), and Raviv (1979).[3] The fundamental problem of optimal insurance is usually developed within the context of a representative consumer who maximizes a von Neumann-Morgenstern (1944) utility function under conditions of uncertainty.

Consider a simple case of a risk-averse agent that faces two uncertain states:

3. Laffont (1989) provides an excellent summary of the theory of insurance. Our discussion follows his summary.

$$w_1 = W \quad \rightarrow \quad \text{Agent does not suffer a loss}$$
$$w_2 = W - L \quad \rightarrow \quad \text{Agent suffers a loss} \qquad (4\text{--}2)$$

where W = wealth and L = loss. The probability of a loss occurring is exogenous and is denoted by π.

Consider an insurance contract that will collect a premium of α and will pay an agent L when a loss occurs. Assuming that the insurer is risk neutral, that contract costs are zero, and that the insurance market is competitive, the insurance contract must satisfy the zero-profit constraint that:

$$\alpha = \pi L, \qquad (4\text{--}3)$$

where α is the total amount paid by the insured for the insurance contract. Define q to be the price per unit of compensation in the event of a loss (the per unit premium) and z to be the units of insurance purchased. The zero-profit condition implies that $q = \pi$.

The consumer will choose a level of insurance z that maximizes:

$$\max \left[(1 - \pi)U(w_1) + \pi U(w_2) \right] \qquad (4\text{--}4)$$

subject to:
$$w_1 = W - qz$$
$$w_2 = W - L + z - qz$$

The first-order condition implies:

$$(1 - \pi)qU'(W - qz) = \pi(1 - q)U'(W - L + z - qz). \qquad (4\text{--}5)$$

With an actuarially fair premium ($q = \pi$), this implies that:

$$U'(W - qz) = U'(W - L + z - qz), \qquad (4\text{--}6)$$

or that the optimal level of insurance is $z = L$. Thus, in a competitive environment with actuarially fair premiums, risk-averse agents will completely insure. Of course, contractual costs are not zero in reality, and thus rates are above the actuarially fair level and insurance is less than complete.

FIGURE 4–1
OPTIMAL INSURANCE PURCHASES IN A COMPETITIVE MARKET

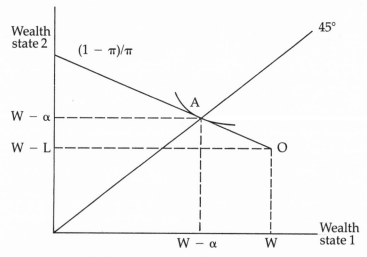

NOTE: See text for definition of variables.
SOURCE: Authors.

The competitive equilibrium is illustrated in figure 4–1. Agents start at an initial endowment of 0, where wealth is equal to W without a loss (state 1) and W-L with a loss (state 2). Consumers may reduce their exposure to risk by trading along the fair-odds line, which has a slope of -$(1-\pi)/\pi$, where π corresponds to the probability of a loss (which is equal to the actuarially fair premium). Given risk aversion, consumers will trade to the point where insurance is complete (point A on the 45° line).

Adverse Selection

Adverse selection may occur if there is heterogeneous risk in the pool. If risk varies across different insurance buyers and the buyers have more information about their likelihood of collecting losses than insurance sellers, adverse selection occurs.[4] Consider a simple case where there are two levels of risk in the pool. Consider two agents who differ only in their probability of suffering a loss. Define π^H and π^L to be the probabilities of losses for the high- and low-risk groups, respectively. Again assume that the insurer sets premiums according to zero-profit conditions. If the insurer is unable to distinguish individual risks, it will charge a common premium rate q, such that:

$$\pi^L < q < \pi^H. \tag{4–7}$$

The high-risk agent chooses z^H to maximize:

$$max\ [\pi^H U(W - L - qz^H + z^H) + (1 - \pi^H)U(W - qz^H)]. \tag{4–8}$$

The first-order conditions imply:

$$\frac{U'(W - L - qz^H + z^H)}{U'(W - qz^H)} = \frac{(1 - \pi^H)q}{\pi^H(1 - q)} \tag{4–9}$$

Likewise, for a low-risk agent:

$$\frac{U'(W - L - qz^L + z^L)}{U'(W - qz^L)} = \frac{(1 - \pi^L)q}{\pi^L(1 - q)} \tag{4–10}$$

Since $\pi^H > \pi^L$, we know that $z^H > z^L$. Thus, with adverse selection, high-risk agents will purchase more insurance. Raising the gross premium rate q will exacerbate this problem since the low-risk agents will compose an ever-decreasing proportion of the insured pool. Low-risk agents may even be priced completely out of the market.

A pooling equilibrium for the case of insurance demand with adverse selection is illustrated in figure 4–2. The low-risk agent faces a much steeper fair-odds

4. Akerlof (1970) provides a detailed intuitive discussion of asymmetrical information and the resulting adverse selection that occurs in a number of different market exchanges.

FIGURE 4–2
Insurance Purchases with Adverse Selection

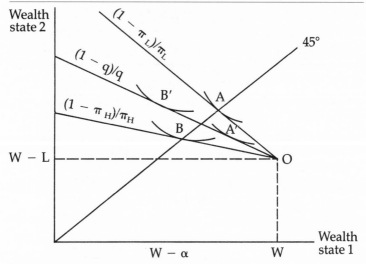

NOTE: See text for definition of variables.
SOURCE: Authors.

line than does the high-risk agent since, by definition, the low-risk agent faces a lower probability of loss. Likewise, the low-risk agent's indifference curve is everywhere (along any ray from the origin) steeper than the high-risk agent's. If the insurer is able to discriminate perfectly between the two groups, actuarially fair rates will be charged in accordance with each group's risk of loss and the competitive solution of complete insurance (points A and B) will again hold for each group. If the insurer is unable to discern individual agent's risk accurately, however, the appropriate actuarially fair rate will lie somewhere between the loss probabilities. In this case, the high-risk agent is undercharged (in accordance with his or her risk of loss) and the low-risk agent is overcharged. The high-risk agent will overpurchase insurance (point B'), and the low-risk agent will underpurchase insurance (point A'). If rates are raised, the low-risk agent will lower his or her insurance purchases at a faster rate than will the high-risk agent. In this way, low-risk agents will have a more elastic demand for insurance than will high-risk agents.[5]

Moral Hazard

Moral hazard extends this problem by allowing the probability of the loss to become endogenized with respect to some effort toward self-protection on the part of agents. Problems arise if the insurer is unable to monitor agents' self-protection efforts and adjust premiums accordingly.

Define x to be the level of self-protection exercised by agents (expressed in monetary units). The endogenous probability of loss is expressed as $\pi(x)$ (where $\pi'(x) < 0$). In this case, the two states of wealth are given by:

$$w_1 = W - x - \pi(x)z \quad \rightarrow \quad \text{Agent does not suffer a loss}$$
$$w_2 = W - x - L - \pi(x)z + z \rightarrow \quad \text{Agent suffers a loss} \quad (4\text{--}11)$$

The consumer chooses x and z to maximize:

$$max \ [(1 - \pi(x))U(w_1) + \pi(x)U(w_2)]$$

subject to:
$$w_1 = W - x - \pi(x)z,$$
$$w_2 = W - x - L - \pi(x)z + z, \text{ and}$$
$$x \geq 0. \quad (4\text{--}12)$$

The first order conditions are:

$$[U(w_2)-U(w_1)]\pi'(x)-\pi(x)(1+\pi'(x))U'(w_2)-$$
$$(1-\pi(x))(1+\pi'(x)z)U'(w_1) = 0,$$

---

5. This result is consistent with Rothschild and Stiglitz's (1977) finding that second-best "self-selection" contracts, under which insured agents incompletely reveal information about the riskiness of their operations, are potentially feasible in private insurance markets in which insurance pools are adversely selected. Nelson and Loehman have suggested, on the basis of the Rothschild-Stiglitz argument, that private all-risk crop insurance markets are not necessarily infeasible.

$$\pi(x)[1-\pi(x)]U'(w_2)-$$
$$[1-\pi(x)]\pi(x)U'(w_1) = 0. \qquad (4\text{--}13)$$

The second condition implies that $U'(w_1) = U'(w_2)$, which implies that $z = L$, or that insurance is again complete.

The solution breaks down, however, if the insurer is unable to observe x and thus charges an exogenous premium q instead of $\pi(x)$. Assume that the per unit premium q is independent of the level of self-protection. The maximization problem becomes:

$$max\ [(1 - \pi(x))U(W - x - zq) + \pi(x)U(W - x - L + z(1 - q))] \qquad (4\text{--}14)$$

The first-order conditions are:

$$\pi'(x)[U(w_2) - U(w_1)] - \pi(x)U'(w_1) -$$
$$(1 - \pi(x))U'(w_2) \le 0\ (= 0\ \text{if}\ x > 0),$$
$$\pi(x)(1 - q)U'(w_2) - (1 - \pi(x))qU'(w_1) = 0. \qquad (4\text{--}15)$$

The second condition implies that $U'(w_1) = U'(w_2)$, or that insurance is complete. Using this fact, we can simplify the first equation to show:

$$-U'(w_1) \le 0\ (= 0\ \text{if}\ x > 0). \qquad (4\text{--}16)$$

Since we know that $U'(w_1)$ must be greater than zero, we know that $x = 0$ is the optimal solution. If an agent's degree of self-protection cannot be observed by the insurer and individual premium rates do not reflect self-protection, agents will choose zero self-protection.

The Transition to an Empirical Framework

A number of extensions to this framework are often undertaken to put the demand problem into an empirical framework. Most often, the transition to an empirical framework for evaluating the demand for insurance by agents who produce under uncertainty typically involves the maximization of expected utility in a mean-variance context. This transition is usually made by adopting one of a number of simplifying assumptions to put the problem in a mean-variance context. The first approach is to assume a constant absolute risk-aversion coefficient ϕ_i (that is, assume a negative exponential-type utility function per Freund [1956]) and thus derive expected utility maximization at the point where:

$$max\ E(\pi_i) - \phi_i \sigma^2_{\pi i}/2. \qquad (4\text{--}17)$$

This is the approach followed by Just and Calvin (1990). Alternatively, one may choose to assume that the outcomes are distributed normally. In this case, the odd-numbered moments of the distribution are zero, and the even-numbered moments are functions of the variance. This allows an infinite-order Taylor's series expansion of the utility function to be expressed as a function of the mean, variance, and risk-aversion coefficient. Finally, it is often assumed that a second-order Taylor's series expansion (making expected utility a function of mean and variance only) is sufficient to represent the distribution of returns. In this case, only the first two moments of the distribution (that is, the mean and variance) are relevant. This is the approach followed by Hojjati and Bockstael (1988).

The Supply of Insurance

If one group of agents wants, and is able, to purchase a certain type of insurance, then another group of agents must be willing to sell it. Adam Smith, in *The Wealth of Nations*, pointed out that for the supplier of insurance (the insurer) to be willing to provide protection to the insured individual, "[the] premium must be sufficient to compensate the common losses, to pay the expense of management, and to afford such a profit as might have been drawn from an equal capital employed in any common trade." All that is required for the insurance to be sold is that the insured be willing to purchase the insurance at that premium. Only if the premium is too high will the insurance not be sold. The facts that private insurance companies have never successfully offered multiple-peril crop insurance contracts and that the U.S. government has to provide substantial premium subsidies to get farmers to participate in its MPCI program indicate that the required actuarially sound premium is too high.

Borch (1989, 13–14) noted that Adam Smith's observation implies that an insurance premium offered by a private insurer, P_p, has three components: E, the expected claim payment (or expected indemnity); A, the administrative expense of the insurance company; and R, the required return on invested capital. That is,

$$P_p = E + A + R. \tag{4–18}$$

In equation 4–18, the expected indemnity, E, is simply the average payout on the insurance contract. If the contract of interest were for annual automobile insurance for, say, a Ford Taurus in New York City owned by a 35-year-old, nonsmoking accountant with a clean driving record, E would simply be the average amount paid in claims under such a contract in that area. The terms A and R represent the insurer's costs of doing business and are often jointly referred to as the loading factor, $L = A + R$.

The loading factor, L, plays a crucial role in determining whether a market for a particular type of insurance will exist. Risk-averse individuals will buy insurance contracts when the premium, $E + L$, is greater than the expected indemnity, E, but not when the difference, L, is too great. They are willing to pay for the income-smoothing service provided by the insurer, but their willingness to pay for any given level of risk reduction is finite. If the loading factor becomes too large, private markets for a given type of insurance will not exist. The loading factor has two elements, R and A. We will consider the determinants of each of these elements in turn.

One element of the loading factor, R, is the insurer's required return on invested capital. The insurer may be risk neutral, risk averse, or even risk loving. A risk-averse insurer, in the context of the above premium formula, would require a higher value for R than a risk-neutral insurer.[6] Risk neutrality, or risk-neutrality-like behavior, on the part of an insurer can reasonably be assumed when the insurer can either *pool* or *spread* most or all the risks associated with an insurance contract. *Risk pooling* (the law of large numbers) is possible when the insurer offers insurance contracts of about the same size to a large number of insured individuals whose individual risks of loss are statistically independent of each other. By pooling such risks, an insurer can reduce the variance of the claims from the insurance pool to almost zero and set premiums without regard to risk of poolwide losses that exceed poolwide premium payments. In this case, the insurer acts as a risk-neutral agent because all individual risk has been pooled away.

Risk pooling is probably not feasible in the case of multiple-peril crop insurance contracts because crop losses are often driven by weather-related events such as drought and floods or pest infestations and disease that are geographically extensive. Such events cause widespread losses among many insured farmers in the insurance pool and are *systemic risks* that the insurer cannot avoid by pooling. Losses among farmers are not independent but positively correlated and, in these circumstances, in any given year the insurance company faces a considerable risk that poolwide losses will exceed poolwide premiums by a substantial amount. *Risk spreading*, however, is possible in these circumstances. While in any given year the farm sector as a whole may experience a substantial loss because of crop failure, in an economy such as that in the United States, where crop production represents a small fraction (less than 1 percent) of total economic activity, the risk of loss can be

---

6. A risk-loving insurer would require an even lower R than a risk-neutral insurer.

spread over the rest of the economy.[7] An insurance company with multiple lines of business (automobile insurance, life insurance, marine and other business insurance, and the like), for example, can spread the risk of large agricultural losses among its other types of business so that the cost of the risk falls to about zero (Layard and Walters 1978).

Rather than diversifying their book of business, insurance companies often specialize in specific lines because each type of business requires specialized knowledge. This failure to diversify leads to managerial diseconomies of scale. In this case, however, insurance companies can still practice risk spreading through the use of reinsurance markets. In reinsurance markets, individuals or firms accept some or all the risks of large losses that an individual company takes on in specializing in a specific type of coverage, in return for premiums that cover expected losses and loading factors. By accepting such risks from many different types of specific insurers, the reinsurers are able both to spread and to pool the risks of losses in a particular sector of the economy across many individuals, reducing the cost of risk to close to zero for both the specific insurance company and the individuals it insures.

Reinsurance is quite feasible for actuarially fair crop insurance contracts. A priori, there is no reason to presume that insurance companies require a high loading factor for multiple-peril crop insurance because the crop sector experiences exceptionally large systemic risks. Nevertheless, reinsurance requires the use of real resources and therefore does increase the administrative component of the loading factor, A, for that type of insurance. Innovations such as the proposal by Miranda and Glauber to develop options markets based on area-yield

7. In fact, country-specific risks can be, and often are, spread over the world economy through international reinsurance markets.

contracts that may reduce the costs of reinsurance for crop insurance companies are therefore potentially welfare enhancing.

Moral hazard, which also affects the administrative cost of the loading factors for crop insurance contracts, is probably more important in deterring private markets for multiple-crop insurance. Borch (1982b) has shown that when moral hazard is a problem, in most circumstances insurers will have to increase their premiums by at least the amount it costs to monitor the insured individual to prevent behavior that increases risk of loss. He also showed that premiums will be increased by more than these monitoring costs when insured individuals refuse to accept large penalties for violations of moral-hazard clauses or, for some reason, it is infeasible to institute such penalties. Borch's result has powerful implications for multiple-peril crop insurance contracts since it is extremely expensive to monitor a farm's behavior during the entire growing season for moral-hazard violations. Such violations, for example, could be as simple as failing to spray for pests when pests are first observed in the fields. Unless the monitor is in the fields almost as often as the farmer, such behavior will be almost impossible to detect. High monitoring costs imply correspondingly high administrative costs and loading factors for insurance contracts. Thus, moral hazard is likely to be a major reason for the failure of private multiple-peril crop insurance contracts.

One type of penalty often proposed as a means of dealing with moral-hazard problems is a large deductible. A deductible is an amount subtracted from the total reported loss before payment is made. If, for example, I have a $250 deductible on my homeowner's insurance and a thief steals my golf clubs, valued at $650 for insurance purposes, I receive an indemnity of only $400 (the total loss less the deductible). The argument for large deductibles in the case of crop insurance is as follows. If farms receive indemnities only when they experience very large losses, their incentives for moral-hazard behavior that increases the likelihood of small losses (through reducing fertilizer or pesticide use) are correspondingly smaller. The problem with requiring large deductibles, however, is that it also reduces the benefits of buying insurance to the insured farm and reduces demand-side incentives for the creation of such a market (Chambers).

Another potential approach to resolving the moral-hazard problem associated with crop insurance is the use of multiyear contracts (Gardner and Kramer 1986). Rubenstein and Yaari (1983) have shown that if insurance contracts have infinitely long lives, moral-hazard problems can be eliminated for full-coverage contracts if, once cheating is detected, the insurer refuses to cover any future losses. Chambers (1989), however, has pointed out that the moral-hazard problem reappears at the end of a finite multiyear contract in the last period, since the insurer has no future recourse against the insured farmer and therefore no credible threat to enforce honest behavior. Nevertheless, at least during a multiyear contract, if penalties for "shirking" are sufficiently high, moral-hazard problems are likely to be mitigated (Chambers 1989; Lambert 1983; and Rogerson 1985). Vercammen and Van Kooten (1994) have shown that, in the absence of premium penalties subsequent to insurance claims, when farmers can control production levels with some degree of certainty, dynamic "cycling" moral-hazard behavior may occur: that is, farmers deliberately increase production in some years and reduce production in others to obtain higher indemnities. Premium penalties that mitigate incentives for such behavior can be imposed only if multiyear contracts are either explicitly or implicitly required by the insurer.

When moral-hazard problems raise loading factors, lead to high deductibles, or result in stringent contracts that impose large penalties for violations of the terms of agreement, the incentives for the creation of insurance markets are diminished. It should also be recognized that moral hazard is not, as such, a market failure but a market condition. There is no reason to suppose that government intervention will remove incentives for moral hazard unless the government has access to lower-cost monitoring devices than do private insurance companies. To our knowledge, no one has suggested that such is the case.

The U.S. government does in fact offer multiple-peril crop insurance to farmers through the FCIC. Over the 1980s, between 20 and 40 percent of total eligible crop acres has been voluntarily insured by farmers, and for more than forty years the government has not required farmers to sign multiyear contracts. The premiums charged by the FCIC do not, however, bear any relation to the premiums that would have to be charged by a private insurance company. Under the terms of the 1980 Federal Crop Insurance Act, the government underwrites all administrative costs and subsidizes almost all losses through its role as reinsurer of the contracts sold by private companies. In effect, the actual premium charged to farmers under the current multiple-peril program is:

$$P_g = (1 - s) E, \tag{4-19}$$

where E is the expected loss and s is the government subsidy per dollar of expected loss. Total government subsidies (the difference between expression 4–18 and expression 4–19) amount to $sE + A + R$ and have been large. Miranda has pointed out that, during the 1980s, total program costs, $E + A + R$, were about twice the total premiums paid by farmers and the effective total premium subsidy $(P_g/P_p = P_g/(E+A+R))$ averaged about 50 percent. In the 1990s, as losses have risen steadily, the total effective premium subsidy has also increased.

The contrast between the private sector's failure to develop viable multiple-peril contracts and its success in offering specific-peril crop insurance against hail and fire was emphasized in the discussion of the history of crop insurance. The reason for the differential involvement of the private sector in those lines of business can now be understood in the context of moral-hazard monitoring costs. Claims for indemnities against the specific perils of fire and hail can be monitored inexpensively, and so the loading factor for such specific-peril crop insurance is much lower than for multiple-peril crop insurance. The viability of commercial specific-peril crop insurance has led to proposals for drought insurance to be triggered by measurable events such as annual or monthly precipitation. While such insurance contracts would reduce loading factors on the supply side, they would also probably provide farmers with less protection because indemnities would be less closely linked to actual yield losses. Some analysts (for example, Quiggin 1986; and Patrick 1988) have presented evidence that Australian wheat farmers are willing to pay quite large amounts for such protection. Bardsley et al. (1984), however, reported that loading factors of even as little as 9 percent would deter such farmers from purchasing rainfall insurance.[8] The actual behavior of insurance companies and theoretical considerations both, then, indicate that unsubsidized commercial multiple-peril crop insurance is probably not a viable commercial product.

---

8. Typically, in most lines of insurance, the loading factor accounts for about 30–40 percent of the total premium paid by the insured individual.

5
A Review of Empirical Research

The empirical literature on crop insurance issues has expanded almost exponentially since the mid-1980s but has had a surprisingly long history, especially with respect to analyses of the demand for crop insurance by farmers initiated in the 1940s. In this chapter, we review the findings and implications of empirical research in three areas: (1) the demand for multiple-peril crop insurance; (2) the viability of multiple-peril and area-yield crop insurance in purely private markets; and (3) the willingness of private insurers to supply federally subsidized multiple-peril crop insurance under existing and potential contractual arrangements.

Empirical studies of the demand for crop insurance have been viewed as important by policy makers for two somewhat contradictory reasons. First, the MPCI program has been plagued with relatively low participation rates, and policy makers have wanted to know why. Second, policy makers have also wanted to know whether raising premiums would be a viable way of reducing losses and loss ratios. As we show below, the answer to the first question is multifaceted. Many variables appear to influence a farmer's decision to purchase crop insurance—premium rates, variability of yields, availability of disaster payments, degree of diversification across crops and livestock operations, and the like—but the fundamental reason is probably that without large subsidies crop insurance is not worth much to farmers. The answer to the second question appears to be more ambiguous because, as premium rates are increased, the insured pool probably becomes more adversely selected and measurably smaller.

While policy makers in the United States have largely chosen not to address the empirical issue of whether private all-risk crop insurance markets are viable, several research studies have investigated the question. The findings of these studies, which are reviewed in the second part of this chapter, indicate that unsubsidized commercial markets are probably not viable, either for multiple-peril crop insurance or area-yield insurance. Finally, empirical results concerning the willingness of private insurers to market multiple-peril crop insurance are reviewed. The evidence suggests that recent changes in marketing methods may cause farmers in some high-loss regions of the country to have great difficulty in purchasing the crop insurance contracts they have elected in previous years.

The Demand for Insurance

In light of the recent problems of low participation (20.77 percent in the 1980s) and poor actuarial performance (a loss ratio in excess of 2.0 for the period covering 1985–1993), demand issues are of central importance to understanding the actuarial performance of the current program and possible alternatives.[1] In particular, com-

1. An excellent survey of the early research addressing demand issues is contained in Gardner and Kramer (1986). Our discussion of this early research is largely a summary of their review.

prehension of the effects of proposed changes requires knowledge of how producers respond to various characteristics of the program, including premium rates. Further, comprehending the interaction between the crop insurance program and ASCS ad hoc disaster relief programs requires an understanding of how disaster relief influences farmers' demand for insurance.

The demand for insurance, often expressed as program participation, has received considerable empirical attention in recent years. Most of the early research that addressed crop insurance issues, however, focused on supply. Much of this research (see, for example, Sanderson [1943]) identified adverse selection as a major problem in the FCIC contracts at that time.

One of the earliest analyses of demand issues was a study by Clendenin (1942). Clendenin evaluated participation in the crop insurance program using surveys from a number of states. He found that small farms with poor financial standing were more likely to participate in the insurance program and that farmers in high-risk areas were less likely to insure because of higher rates in such areas. Using county-level aggregated data, he also found that county premium rates and participation were inversely correlated. This is the first evidence that farmers were indeed sensitive to premium rates (that is, that the elasticity of demand for insurance is negative). Finally, Clendenin found that tenants and diversified farms were more likely to insure.

Two early master's theses from the University of Nebraska evaluated the attitudes of FCIC participants. Bray (1963) found that most participants favored higher levels of coverage and indicated that they would be willing to pay higher premiums for such coverage. Bray also found that obtaining insurance appeared to aid in obtaining credit. Starr (1963) found that many farmers believed that increasing trends in yields brought about inadequate coverage in the FCIC program.

Jones and Larson (1965) used survey data from Virginia and Montana to evaluate differences between insurance buyers and nonbuyers. They found that insured farmers were less diversified, less likely to have irrigation, and more highly leveraged. They also found that agricultural lenders reported better loan performance for insured producers.

Characteristics of insurance buyers versus nonbuyers were evaluated by the Great Plains Regional Research Project GP-8. In Loftsgard's summary (1967) of a survey of farmers' insurance attitudes and purchases, he found few significant differences between program participants and nonparticipants. The only consistent differences he reported were that participants tended to be older and more dependent on cash-grain income than nonparticipants.

Shipley (1967) evaluated characteristics of participants and nonparticipants among northwest Texas farmers. Participation was found to be significantly higher among farmers with poor water supplies and poor soils. No significant differences in age, education, number of dependents, experience, or yields between participants and nonparticipants were revealed. He found that approximately 50 percent of the farmers indicated that insurance substituted for diversification.

In a survey of east Tennessee farmers, Beeson (1971) found that total income and assets were higher among farmers who did not purchase insurance. Insurance buyers had a higher share of tobacco income and a smaller share of livestock income than nonbuyers. A surprising result was that participants had lower debt levels than nonparticipants. Beeson's results indicated that only 9.4 percent of those farmers who had dropped their insurance did so because premiums were too high. Most had dropped because of insufficient coverage. Because inadequate coverage at a given premium rate can also be interpreted as too high a premium rate for a given level of protection, this distinction, however, may not be relevant.

Recent empirical research has given attention to premium effects on participation. In particular, several recent studies have empirically estimated demand price elasticities. Nieuwoudt et al. (1985) estimated the demand for crop insurance using pooled state-level aggregated data for 1965 to 1981. Their study evaluated participation in the context of insured acreage for corn, wheat, soybeans, and cotton. They found that the expected rate of return to insurance was an important factor explaining participation. A critical component of the expected rate of return to insurance is the premium rate. Thus, the effects of premiums on participation are implicit in expected returns, although Nieuwoudt et al. did not explicitly report an elasticity. They also found that expected yield risk, diversification, crop dominance, tenure, size, and dummy variables for years with disaster relief were significant in explaining participation.

Gardner and Kramer (1986) used fifty-seven county-level observations for 1979 to model the demand for crop insurance. Insurance purchases were represented as the proportion of insurable acreage actually insured for all crops in each county. They found that the expected rate of return to insurance was a significant factor explaining demand. Their results suggested that a subsidy of 30 percent on premiums would increase participation from 20 percent to 25.5 percent, implying an elasticity of -.92. Gardner and Kramer also found that recent returns weighed more heavily in influencing purchases than did earlier experiences. Their results also suggested that tobacco producers and part-owners were more likely to purchase insurance.

Barnett, Skees, and Hourigan (1990) evaluated the demand for insurance in 346 individual wheat-producing counties in thirteen wheat-producing states in 1987.

They used the proportion of insurable acres actually insured as a measure of the quantity of insurance purchased. Their results confirmed the importance of expected returns to insurance as a variable influencing demand. Their study, the first to calculate an explicit demand elasticity, obtained a price elasticity of about -.2. They also found that delivery costs, off-farm income, livestock production, and interest payments were significant factors influencing the demand for crop insurance.

Calvin (1990) used participation data for individual producers to model the demand for insurance in a discrete dependent variable framework. Her results suggested that expected returns to insurance, age, livestock production, government program participation, and leverage were significant factors affecting the discrete decision to purchase insurance.

Goodwin (1993) evaluated the demand for insurance using pooled county-level data for Iowa corn production between 1985 and 1990. In contrast to earlier studies, Goodwin addressed adverse selection and how it might influence producers' responses to changes in premiums. His research was conducted at a time when the FCIC was receiving recommendations to increase premiums across the board to alleviate losses. A General Accounting Office report (1992, 25), for example, noted that "our periodic financial audits...confirm that FCIC has not charged high enough premiums to achieve actuarial soundness." Goodwin found that producers' responsiveness to premium changes was significantly influenced by their risk of loss, which he measured using historical average loss ratios for each county. Loss ratios greater than 1 are an important indicator of the presence of adverse selection in the insurance pool. Thus, his results implied that, because of adverse selection, high-risk producers were less responsive to premium changes. Goodwin used two distinct measures of insurance purchases: the proportion of insurable acres actually insured and liability per insurable acre. He argued that, because insurance contracts offered various levels of yield and price elections, farmers could respond by changing these elections without dropping coverage altogether and thus that liability gave a more realistic representation of purchases than insured acres. Goodwin obtained elasticity estimates of -0.32 for insured acres and -0.73 for liability, thus confirming that liability had a more elastic response to premiums. His results showed that these elasticities varied from relatively elastic responses for low-risk producers to inelastic responses for risky producers. Goodwin's simulation of the effects of across-the-board premium increases suggested that such policy changes would increase revenues collected from producers but would also increase the riskiness of the insurance pool, as low-risk producers cancel coverage faster than high-risk producers.

A limitation of Goodwin's (1993) analysis of the demand for insurance is his use of county-level aggregate data. Aggregation errors and biases undoubtedly influence empirical estimates of elasticities and related parameters. Goodwin notes that, because aggregation decreases variation, the effects of adverse selection may be even greater than those suggested in his analysis. In addition, Hartman (1982, 1983) has shown that cross-sectional aggregation may induce errors in variables that results in a bias toward zero in parameter estimates. Thus, the effects of policy changes, such as across-the-board premium changes, might be even greater than would be suggested by empirical estimates garnered from county-level data.

Smith and Baquet (1993) avoided this limitation by using individual producer-level data for insurance purchases by Montana wheat producers. Their results indicate a demand elasticity of about -0.60. Their results also suggest that, because of adverse selection, this elasticity differs with risk of loss and that the nature of this difference depends on whether the farm has a positive or a negative expected return from insurance. For farms with positive expected returns, demand becomes more elastic as risk of loss rises. The opposite result is obtained for farms with negative expected returns.

Goodwin (1994) investigated the demand for insurance using data from a survey of individual wheat producers in Kansas. He included a variable that represented farmers' perceptions regarding the degree of protection against catastrophic yield losses that they were provided by ad hoc ASCS disaster relief programs. His results confirmed that farmers who perceived themselves to be protected by disaster relief programs were much less likely (16 percent less likely) to purchase crop insurance.

Coble, Knight, Pope, and Williams (1993) modeled the demand for multiple-peril crop insurance by Kansas wheat producers. Their results implied a demand elasticity of -0.26 (with demand measured by participation) and also suggested that producers may be more responsive to subsidy changes than premium changes. They explain this effect as a result of farmers' greater awareness of subsidy changes than net premium changes.

In all, the existing empirical studies of the demand for insurance agree on several points. First, the demand for insurance seems to be inelastic, at least for the average producer. Table 5–1 summarizes demand elasticity estimates from a number of studies. These estimates range from -0.20 (Barnett, Skees, and Hourigan 1990) to -0.90 (Gardner and Kramer 1986). Several of the studies allow this elasticity to vary with a measure of the risk of loss to model the effects of adverse selection explicitly. This approach consistently confirms that low-risk producers have a more elastic demand. Only very low-risk producers, however, are found to have an elastic response to premium changes. A second important result summarized from these studies is that the elasticity of demand for insurance varies significantly for different crops in differ-

TABLE 5–1
SUMMARY OF EMPIRICAL ESTIMATES OF CROP INSURANCE
DEMAND ELASTICITIES, 1986–1993

Study	Crops	Elasticity
Goodwin (1993)	Iowa corn	-.73 for liability
		-.32 for acres
Goodwin & Kastens (1993)	Kansas wheat	-.51 for liability
Gardner & Kramer (1986)	U.S. crops	-.92 for acres
Barnett, Skees, & Hourigan (1990)	U.S. crops	-.20 for acres
Smith and Baquet (1993)	Montana wheat	-.58 to -.69 for liability
Coble et al. (1993)	Kansas wheat	-.26 for participation

NOTE: Goodwin, Goodwin and Kastens, and Smith and Baquet show that elasticity varies inversely with the risk of loss.
SOURCE: Authors.

ent regions. Recognition of this variation is essential for policy makers' effective formulation of future policies. Recent research (Barnett and Skees 1994) suggests that existing point estimates from individual crops or regions could form the basis for setting future policies. The variation in empirical findings among different crops and regions, however, suggests that national policy should not be based on a single set of empirical results obtained for an individual crop in a particular state or region.

Across-the-Board Rate Increases, a Way to Lower Losses?

Several recent analyses of insurance demand point out that adverse selection causes high-risk producers to be less responsive to changes in premium rates than low-risk producers. This observation implies that across-the-board rate increases will result in a riskier insurance pool.

According to recent research (Barnett, Skees, and Hourigan 1990; Barnett and Skees 1994), evidence that the demand for insurance is inelastic lends support for across-the-board rate increases as a means for improving the actuarial performance of the program. They demonstrate that if demand is inelastic for the average producer, loss ratios must fall as premiums are increased across the board. A similar recommendation has been made by GAO, which stated that "periodic financial audits confirm...that FCIC has not charged high enough premiums to achieve actuarial soundness" (1992, 25).

A prudent examination of the empirical evidence and its limitations suggests that across-the-board premium increases may be, in the best case, a suboptimal policy recommendation and, in the worst case, actually damaging to the actuarial performance of the program. First, as noted above, estimates of demand elasticity appear to differ significantly across crops and regions. Policy recommendations based on an elasticity estimate from a particular crop in a specific region may worsen the actuarial performance of the program for other crops in other regions. A more subtle limitation of much of our knowledge about the elasticity of demand for crop insurance is that most studies have used aggregate data. But cross-sectional aggregation of the sort applied in most demand studies may bias elasticity estimates toward zero. In similar analyses of household energy demand, Hartman (1982, 1983) showed that this sort of cross-sectional aggregation resulted in a measurement error that biased price elasticity estimates toward zero. The demand for insurance may thus be more elastic than suggested by studies using aggregate data.

Finally, and most important, even if one is confident that demand is inelastic, across-the-board premium changes provide only a second-best correction for the adverse-selection problems that have led to significant program losses. While it may be possible to reduce losses by increasing premiums across the board, a superior solution could certainly be obtained from refinements in rate-setting techniques that addressed adverse selection. In this light, recommendations to increase all premiums to lower losses may mislead policy makers' efforts to improve the actuarial performance of the program.

Empirical Evidence regarding Moral Hazard

Conventional wisdom has long held that farmers' moral-hazard actions typically come about when insured farmers reduce agricultural inputs. The conventional wisdom is that insured farmers will use fewer inputs in an attempt to increase their likelihood of collecting indemnities. In this light, crop insurance programs have often been viewed as being "environmentally friendly" in that they are perceived to lower applications of agricultural chemicals. In a recent challenge to this view, Quiggin (1994) noted that it is theoretically possible for moral hazard to increase the dispersion (variance) of crop yields. The notion is that some inputs are "risk increasing." Horowitz and Lichtenberg (1993) extended this idea in an empirical analysis of insurance demand and use of inputs. According to their results, farmers who purchased insurance tended to use more agricultural chemicals than uninsured producers. In particular, they found that pesticide use and nitrogen applications were larger for farms that purchased insurance. Such evidence, which conflicts with the popular perceptions about the environmental effects of the crop insurance program, has generated considerable discussion. Smith and Goodwin (1994) discuss several limitations of the modeling approach pursued by Horowitz and Lichtenberg (1993), which may explain the inconsistency of their results with conventional wisdom. A principal reason identified by Smith and Goodwin for the unexpected conclusions reached by Horowitz and Lichtenberg is their failure to recognize the joint decision-making process involved in insurance purchases and chemical applications. Smith and Goodwin maintain that this limitation leads to a significant bias, which results in insured farmers appearing to use more inputs rather than less. Smith and Goodwin explicitly model the decision to use inputs and to purchase insurance simultaneously for Kansas wheat producers and find that insured producers use significantly less chemical inputs than do uninsured producers. In particular, insured producers appear to spend an average of $4.75 less per acre on chemical inputs than do uninsured producers.

A meaningful consideration of the effects of input use on insurance decisions requires a reliable definition of *risk*. Vague notions that define an input to be "risk increasing" solely because it increases the variation of yields may be misleading, or even invalid in an economic context. A simple example illustrates this point. Corn yields might average 120 bushels per acre and have a standard deviation of 20 bushels per acre. Wheat yields might have an average of 30 bushels per acre and a standard deviation of 10 bushels per acre. A consideration of variance suggests that corn is indeed the "riskier" crop because its variance is twice as large. No sensible comparison, however, would lead to such a conclusion. If the scale effect is removed by deflating variance (or the standard deviation) by the mean, one obtains a more reasonable measure of yield risk: the coefficient of variation (CV). In this example, corn has a CV of 16.7 percent, while wheat has a CV of 33.3 percent. While this scale effect seems intuitively obvious, its recognition is critical for a correct comprehension of the effects of decisions on use of inputs. Chemical inputs may indeed increase the variance of yields, but the effect of such a change on yield "risk" is uncertain without a joint consideration of changes in expected yields (means). One would expect increases in inputs, at least small changes local to conventional levels of use, to bring about increases in expected yields. Without considering this scale effect on the first moment of the distribution, we cannot make valid inferences about risk.

This does not imply that risk should be represented by the coefficient of variation for yields. The risk to yield may not be the variable relevant to input use and insurance decisions. Rather, producers are more likely to be concerned with the net revenue effects (first, second, and higher moments) of such decisions. In this context, a valid consideration of the risk effects of input and insurance decisions must include the increased costs of increased use of inputs. Even if increasing the use of inputs raises the probability that a producer will collect insurance indemnities, this increase in expected returns must be weighed against the increased production costs of increasing inputs.

Are Private Markets for Crop Insurance Viable?

The question of whether private insurance markets for multiple-peril or rainfall crop insurance are feasible has been addressed by a series of papers (Bardsley et al. 1984; Quiggin 1986; Patrick 1988; and Fraser 1988), largely in the context of Australian wheat production. Bardsley et al. consider an insurance scheme under which farmers in a given area receive indemnities if the area is deemed to have experienced a drought. Farmers and insurers are assumed to be equally risk averse, but because the estimated correlation coefficient between yields across areas is less than 1, some risk pooling is possible. Under these assumptions, Bardsley et al. show that in New South Wales such a private insurance contract is infeasible even when administrative costs are very low (less than 10 percent of total premiums) and farmers are quite risk averse.

In a comment on the analysis by Bardsley et al. (1984), Quiggin (1986) argued that the barriers to such an area-yield insurance program had been overstated. Quiggin suggested that insurers with a large portfolio of unrelated risks would act as if they were risk neutral. Imposing risk aversion on insurers was therefore inappropriate and implicitly amounted to increasing administrative costs to disproportionately high levels. Quiggin therefore concluded that drought (or rainfall) area-yield insurance was a potentially viable product. As Quiggin also noted, however, if the product were commercially viable and opportunities for profits were available to insurers, why did such an insurance contract not already exist?

The willingness of wheat producers in the Australian Mallee River valley to pay for two types of crop insurance was examined by Patrick (1988). Sixty producers were provided with details of a U.S.-type of multiple-peril crop insurance and an area-yield contract under which payments would be triggered by rainfall. Assuming that loading factors similar to those used by private insurers for Australian fire and hail contracts (about 30 percent of premiums) would be charged, Patrick concluded that, in an area in which production risk for wheat is as great as anywhere in the United States, "twenty percent or less of the producers would be willing to pay the estimated full costs of the insurance programs."

Fraser (1988) also adopted a willingness-to-pay approach to examine the likely participation of farmers in multiple-peril crop insurance schemes. He did not use survey data but instead assumed an underlying mean-variance expected utility framework in which the farmer's utility depends on income. A range of assumptions about the parameters of the farmer's utility function and the distributions of prices and yields was used to obtain estimates of farmers' willingness to pay for crop insurance. Fraser's results also indicated that if loading factors for multiple-peril crop insurance are similar to those assumed by Patrick (which are representative of loading factors common across all commercial insurance lines), then private multiple-peril crop insurance would be purchased by very few farmers. Only if loading factors were atypically low (between 2 and 10 percent of total premiums) would private MPCI markets be viable.

The empirical evidence on the viability of either area-yield or multiple-peril crop insurance seems to be clear. When normal commercial loading factors are applied, the premiums required by insurers to offer an actuarially viable private crop insurance contract are sufficiently high to reduce the demand for such contracts to zero. Only if implausibly low loading factors are assumed and farmers are highly risk averse are private markets for either type of contract viable. Because moral-hazard problems are likely to be quite severe for multiple-peril contracts, monitoring costs are likely to create loading factors that are atypically large, not atypically small. Thus, private markets for multiple-peril crop insurance are almost surely infeasible, and the weight of the empirical evidence indicates that area-yield contracts are also not commercially viable (in part because, as Patrick's results and findings by Smith et al. [1994] indicate, such contracts offer smaller benefits to producers than do individual-yield contracts).

The Supply of Multiple-Peril Crop Insurance under the Current Program

Since 1981, multiple-peril crop insurance contracts have been marketed by private insurance agents under two types of contracts: master marketer contracts and private reinsurance contracts. Under a master marketing contract, an insurance agent sold MPCI contracts in return for a fixed percentage of the total premiums generated by those sales. The master marketer's responsibilities ended, however, once the farmer signed the insurance contract; adjusting losses and paying indemnities then became the responsibility of the FCIC. Under a reinsurance contract, an insurance company not only markets MPCI contracts but also assesses losses and pays indemnities. The insurance company is then reimbursed for most, but not necessarily all, of its indemnity payments through free reinsurance from the federal government.

The provisions of the reinsurance contract require that some risk of loss be borne by the private insurance company. If losses on the company's book of business exceed indemnities by more than a predetermined proportion (typically about 110 percent), then the private insurer is required to pay a small percentage (typically about 2 percent) of the additional losses. The share of total losses to be paid by the private insurer is, however, capped at about 10 percent of total premiums or one-third of the private insurer's income.

The amount of risk exposure faced by the reinsurance companies is very small compared with the risk exposure of normal commercial insurance contracts. Crop insurance companies operating under reinsurance contracts, however, do confront some risk of loss and may, in the future, have to bear a larger portion of total risk of loss. They will also be the sole vehicle for providing farmers with MPCI coverage in 1995–1996 as master marketing contracts have been phased out.

The fact that private insurers do have to bear some risk raises several empirical issues. Will private insurers, for example, seek to avoid selling MPCI contracts in regions in which losses have been high relative to premiums? Smith and Kehoe (1994) showed that, under the existing reinsurance contract, private insurers will tend to avoid high-loss regions if the actuarial link between premiums and expected losses is weak (that is, when expected losses per hundred dollars of coverage rise by a dollar, premiums rise by substantially less than a dollar) but that they will be willing to serve such areas if the actuarial link is strong. When Smith and Kehoe examined the empirical link between premium rates and expected losses across counties in Montana in 1992, however, they found that premiums rose by only about ten cents when expected losses per hundred dollars of coverage increased by a dollar. They also presented empirical results showing that the probability that farmers purchased MPCI under private reinsurance contracts fell when expected losses increased across counties. Thus, some farmers may face considerable difficulty in purchasing the MPCI coverage they want in the future. In addition, if the reinsurance contract is altered to increase the proportion of losses paid for by private insurers, as has been urged by the General Accounting Office, then this problem will be exacerbated.[2]

One way of mitigating the effects of any increase in the private insurer's risk of loss is to develop low-cost ways in which the insurer can reinsure its crop insurance book of business in the private market. Using information on the 1993 books of business of ten large private crop insurers, Miranda and Glauber (1994) showed that state-based area-yield insurance options contracts may be able to reduce the riskiness of a private crop insurer's entire book of business to levels comparable with those for automobile insurance or homeowner's insurance (areas in which risk pooling removes almost all the risk). If,

2. The crop insurance reform measures being considered by Congress will allow farms to buy minimum levels of catastrophic coverage from local ASCS offices, but such insurance is almost worthless to most farmers. Meaningful "top up" MPCI coverage would still have to be purchased from private insurers who may be unwilling to market such contracts in high-loss areas if their risk of loss is increased.

then, a subsidized federal MPCI program continues to exist and private reinsurers are to be the only suppliers of the product, one relatively low-cost alternative for ensuring that those companies continue to offer MPCI in all areas might be to subsidize their costs of obtaining reinsurance through such options contracts.

6
Alternative Crop Insurance Programs

Many proposals for crop insurance reform have perco-
lated through recent debates over the viability of current
U.S. federal crop insurance and disaster relief programs.
In the first part of this chapter, we examine several widely
discussed alternative programs, including revenue insurance and revenue assurance (the Iowa plan), independent
insurance for prices and for yields, cost-of-production insurance, target price put options coupled with replacement value and yield insurance, and rainfall insurance
contracts. Many of these programs, in one guise or another, have been implemented in other countries. Thus,
in the second part of this chapter, we review the international record of government-sponsored crop and revenue
insurance programs. The findings are somewhat grim.
Generally, none of these programs has been successful (in
terms of farmer participation) unless farmers' premiums
have been heavily subsidized by taxpayers.

Alternatives to the Current Program

A number of alternatives to the current federal crop insurance program have been proposed, including various

forms of revenue insurance and cost-of-production insurance. Several of these proposals, such as notions of revenue insurance, are modeled after existing programs in other countries (for example, Canada's Gross Revenue Insurance Program). As is the case with the current federal program, each of the various alternatives faces its own limitations and difficulties with respect to implementation. The following discussion describes the alternative proposals and the potential shortcomings and limitations associated with each of them.

Revenue Insurance and Revenue Assurance

A number of proposals for some form of revenue "insurance" or "assurance" have recently surfaced in the debate over farm policies. One such proposal is the plan put forward by Harrington and Doering (1993) to provide gross revenue insurance by insuring price and yield separately. Yield coverage would be offered through a conventional form of crop insurance, while price shortfalls would be paid out of a separate insurance fund. The Revenue Assurance Plan advocated by the Iowa 1995 Farm Bill Study Team (1994) is another alternative that would provide joint price and yield protection. Still other alternatives that make use of existing options markets have been recently proposed by Barnaby (1994).

A potential weakness inherent in current methods for insuring price (in futures markets) and yield (through crop insurance markets) involves the correlation between price and yields. When yield shortfalls are widespread, the resulting decline in marketwide production tends to increase prices. The predicted prices used to specify price elections in the insurance contract do not accurately reflect the true market value of the crop shortfall in years in which market prices may be considerably above insurance guarantees. Various proposals for overcoming this limitation have been put forward, including revenue insurance as well as replacement value contracts under which indemnities are based on prices at harvest. Distinctions between revenue insurance and revenue assurance are often drawn. In general, the most important distinction is that when revenue protection is provided, under insurance plans, premiums are collected from farmers, while, under assurance plans, protection is provided by the government without charge.

The Iowa Revenue Assurance Plan

The 1995 Farm Bill Study Team, sponsored by the Iowa Farm Bureau and other Iowa farm groups, has proposed that current price- and income-support programs, insurance programs, and disaster relief programs be largely replaced by a single revenue assurance program. This program would guarantee farmers 70 percent of "normal" revenues and replace all other government price- and income-support programs. Premiums and administrative costs of the program would be paid by the government. Producers would be free to plant whatever crops they wished. In addition, output levels would be unconstrained, and producers would be free to produce whatever output they desired. Acreage reduction and diversion programs would be eliminated. Over time, farmers would develop yield and revenue histories that would form the basis for insurance.

Advocates of the Iowa plan argue that the plan allows agriculture to be more responsive to market conditions, while lessening the effects of government programs on the marketplace. Because the plan would relax constraints on decisions related to crop planting and, as a result, encourage flexibility in such decisions in response to changes in market conditions, advocates claim that the Iowa plan also clarifies the purpose of farm programs: to protect and support farm incomes. In addition, the Iowa plan is claimed to be neutral with respect to farm size and location in that an identical proportion of revenues is guaranteed to all farmers.

The Iowa farm plan does provide for some "decoupling" of farm programs, a process that economists have encouraged for many years (see, for example, Blandford, DeGorter, Gardner, and Harvey 1990). Decoupling would disconnect agricultural support from production and pricing decisions to minimize the distortionary effects of income-supporting policies. Because farmers are generally allowed to respond to market conditions, production and prices are not distorted, and policy-induced economic inefficiencies are mitigated. Of course, this is a partial equilibrium argument that abstracts from the economywide distortions imposed by the redistribution of welfare into the farm sector.[1]

Probably the most important problem that must be addressed in implementing the Iowa Farm Bill Study Team's proposal is the identification and quantification of "normal" revenues for each farm. In effect, the plan simply assumes that every participating producer has readily available data to establish individual proven yields for all crops (Iowa Farm Bill Study Team 1994). The plan acknowledges (p. 14) that "record keeping becomes a very necessary task" under the program. The FCIC's experience with the federal crop insurance program since 1980, however, is a testimony to the difficulties of setting program benefits on the basis of individual farm records. The limitations of record keeping and maintaining a proven yield for a revenue insurance or assurance program such as the Iowa plan are identical to those that confront the

1. The importance of economywide distortions associated with raising revenues for the efficient choice of agricultural policy instruments has been discussed by (among others) Gardner (1983, 1988); Alston and Hurd (1990); Alston, Carter, and Smith (1993); and Bullock (1994).

current multiple-peril crop insurance program. In addition, as crop mixtures changed with market conditions under the new flexibility afforded by the Iowa plan, expected revenues would also adjust. This shifting would further complicate the determination of normal revenues for the purposes of revenue insurance.

Several other important administrative and implementation issues associated with the Iowa plan have also not been resolved. In addition to the difficulties of identifying expected yields and normal revenues, the determination of program prices and acreage is unclear. Coverage of field crops such as peanuts, tobacco, sugar, cotton, fruits, vegetables, and forage crops remains undefined. Similarly, the Iowa plan provides no clear indications about how adjustments would be made to "normal revenues" for different production practices such as double cropping, summer fallow, irrigation, crop rotations, and conservation improvements. These important issues significantly complicate the feasibility of the Iowa proposal. Tweeten et al. (1994) identified several other problems with the Iowa proposal, noting, for example, that farmers might suffer income and wealth losses as a result of the plan, since the value of program benefits would be lower and land prices would therefore fall. They also pointed out that the program might actually provide moral-hazard incentives for farmers to adopt practices that would increase the variation in their income to strengthen their likelihood of collecting payments. Because revenue is guaranteed only at 70 percent of normal levels, the potential for such moral-hazard effects is unclear and may depend on how normal revenues are determined. The potential for such a problem should at least be acknowledged, however.

The Iowa Farm Bureau proposal, notable for its unique approach to the reform of agricultural policy, is revolutionary in its call for the replacement of all existing policies with a single revenue assurance program. In light of the radical change advocated by the program, the likelihood that such a program would be implemented seems small. Given the trend toward reducing support for agriculture, however, variations of such a program may receive greater attention in future debates about agricultural policy.

The Harrington and Doering Proposal

Harrington and Doering (1993) proposed a form of revenue insurance that would restructure U.S. agricultural programs along the lines of current Canadian revenue insurance programs. Their proposal, which relied heavily on some of the features of the Canadian revenue insurance programs discussed below, set forth two basic provisions: federal crop insurance of the form currently in place and commodity price insurance that would pay farmers when prices fell below a predetermined target. Under the yield insurance proposed by Harrington and Doering, farmers would pay actuarially sound premiums as a requirement of joining the program. Their proposal is, however, extremely vague about how such actuarially fair premiums would be constructed.

Following the provisions of the Canadian programs, Harrington and Doering suggested that shortfalls would be determined by a comparison of market prices against a 10- or 15-year moving average price. Prices that fell below the target (average) would be supported by deficiency payments made out of a revolving fund financed by farmers or by the government. Harrington and Doering demonstrated that their proposal to insure yield and price separately could be used to insure revenues and claimed that the risk-eliminating feature of their program would allow farmers to plan on the basis of a minimum guaranteed revenue level. They also asserted that, with much of the price uncertainty eliminated from farm gross revenue streams, farmers would be able to make better investment and management decisions.

Harrington and Doering's proposal also suffers from the same maladies that afflict the Iowa plan with respect to the feasibility of developing relevant proven yield histories at the farm level. Problems with obtaining accurate information on farm yields has plagued the current federal crop insurance program. In fact, regardless of quality or accuracy, generally obtaining any moderately extended records of histories of farm yields has proved to be difficult. Further, Harrington and Doering's plan states that "farmers would pay actuarially sound premiums" without stating exactly how such premiums would be determined. Clearly, one of the biggest challenges to the construction of an actuarially sound insurance program is calculation of sound premium rates. Stating that such rates would be charged without providing greater details about how the rates would be constructed undermines the credibility of the proposal.

Finally, Barnaby (1994) has noted that the use of a moving average price in a voluntary program such as Harrington and Doering's would allow growers to select into and out of the program adversely on the basis of price trends.[2] During periods of upward trending prices, producers would find it advantageous not to participate in the program. Alternatively, when expected prices are low relative to the ten- or fifteen-year moving average price, farmers would be more likely to participate.

Private Revenue Insurance

Barnaby (1994) has pointed out that many of the instruments necessary for revenue insurance already exist in private markets. He proposes a form of revenue insurance that uses existing options markets to insure price at

2. In fact, Turvey and Chen (1994) have pointed out that Canadian farmers have been opting out of Canadian insurance programs that use a fifteen-year moving average market price because the moving average price has been falling.

a target level and a revised form of crop insurance that replaces yield shortfalls at market value (that is, a replacement endorsement). Under this combination, growers are able to insure their revenue at the target price.

Barnaby notes that current crop insurance does not guarantee bushels but instead guarantees a fixed dollar amount of indemnities. In this way, he notes that farmers who experience losses in periods of high prices (a likely combination of circumstances given the negative correlation between national yields and prices) would receive significantly less in indemnities than their crop was actually worth. Replacement coverage, an endorsement already available in some crop insurance markets, pays indemnities on the basis of market prices at harvest. Replacement coverage has been recommended as a way to reduce moral hazard when prices are very low. Producers who have guaranteed a price for yield shortfalls significantly above market prices may actually find their crop worth more as an insurance loss than as a harvested and sold crop. Replacement value coverage eliminates such a moral-hazard incentive by basing indemnities on market prices.

Under Barnaby's plan, standard multiple-peril crop insurance would include an endorsement that paid indemnities on the basis of actual market prices at harvest. In addition, the government would purchase a put option for each producer at the target price. The government would pay the full premium cost of the target price put option plus basis. Investors would then assume the downside price risk. Producers who received the target price put option with replacement value crop insurance would be guaranteed a minimum level of revenue.

Private companies have offered replacement value endorsements for the past four years. Beginning in the spring of 1994, the FCIC offered catastrophic reinsurance for private companies writing a replacement value endorsement. The availability of such catastrophic reinsurance is expected to lead to a substantial expansion in the number of companies offering replacement endorsements and to increase the number of states in which the contract is available.

Once a replacement endorsement is in place, producers can insure a gross level of revenue simply by maintaining a short futures hedge position. If producers lock in a price through a short hedge and the market price increases, they will receive a margin call. Their insurance coverage increases, however, because yields are insured at replacement value. If the price increase is maintained, the margin money will be lost, but the lost margin is recovered by the higher cash market price. If prices decrease, producers gain in their futures position, but this gain is offset by the crop's lower selling price in the cash market. Barnaby shows that the use of put options will accomplish the same objectives, while eliminating the margin call potential of the futures hedge.

A pilot test program of the target put form of revenue insurance was mandated in 1993–1994 for wheat in two Kansas counties and two North Dakota counties, and for corn in nine counties in the Corn Belt. Wheat growers could choose a September $4.20 put option (at the Kansas City Board of Trade for winter wheat or the Minneapolis Grain Exchange for spring wheat) or the regular deficiency payment. Corn growers could choose a $2.90 put option at the Chicago Board of Trade or the regular deficiency payment. The Chicago Board of Trade proposed an extension of the target price put option for 1994 that would have provided coverage on 10 percent of ASCS program bushels nationwide. The proposal was not accepted, however.

The target put option proposal also faces the same limitations with accurately determining insurable yields as those faced by the current crop insurance program as well as other proposed alternatives for revenue insurance. Accurate individual farm records are necessary to define expected yields. Such a program would presumably make use of current FCIC procedures for determining insurable yields. In this light, the program would be confronted with the same adverse-selection problems on the yield side as those faced by the current federal crop insurance program. Another limitation with the target put proposal is that its coverage is restricted to crops traded in futures markets or that can be effectively cross-hedged with other crops.

An additional concern is that the current size of a target put option is 5,000 bushels. A producer with 7,500 bushels to insure may only be able to insure revenues partially. Alternatively, different pooling or cost-sharing arrangements might be feasible for dividing contracts to offer full coverage. A strength of the proposal for the target put option is that private markets generate the price coverage. In this light, incentives for actuarial soundness are strengthened in that private investors who assume the risk have profit incentives to ensure that options premiums accurately reflect the risk of price changes.

Barnaby's proposed target put option offers a means for combining existing private marketing institutions with government-backed yield insurance to guarantee producers a minimum level of revenues. Although important operational issues need to be resolved, many of the institutions required to implement the program already exist. An essential prerequisite for this semiprivate form of revenue insurance is the availability of replacement value endorsements, which, however, are currently offered only in a few areas.

Cost-of-Production Insurance

Recent initiatives for changes in the current federal crop insurance program have also included a proposal to insure farmers' costs of production. Under such a plan, producers would be guaranteed a certain proportion of their crop production expenses. This proposal is quite similar to the revenue insurance concept, except that target revenues are based on farm-level costs of production rather than on expected farm-level revenues. The belief that underlies calls for such insurance is that producers should be assured of getting back at least their costs of production. Variations on this proposal include a form of insurance where, as is the case in Panama and Brazil, coverage levels would increase throughout the growing season, reflecting the farmer's increased (short-term) investment in the crop.

The obvious shortcoming of this insurance is the difficulty of measuring a farm's production costs. Although detailed budgets for representative farms are often available from cooperative extension sources, the degree to which such budgets could be used to measure actual individual farms' production costs is unclear. A fundamental question is, Whose cost of production should be taken to be representative? Production costs vary significantly over location and even across individual farms within a common geographic region. The average cost of producing a bushel of wheat, collected from 1992 farm records, is $5.03 in northwest Kansas, for example, but only $3.31 in southwest Kansas. Moreover, these are simply average figures for an entire crop-reporting district. The variation in costs becomes much greater with the individual farm. Production costs vary according to individual farm characteristics such as soil type and field slope and elevation. Management practices may also significantly influence actual production costs. How such differences would be resolved in identifying losses and indemnities is unclear. These types of measurement problems are likely to induce adverse selection in such an insurance program. If an aggregate cost-of-production measure were used to define indemnities, low-cost, relatively risky producers could select against the program since their expected returns would exceed those of producers with costs above the area average. Further, such a program may have an additional incentive for moral hazard since less intensive use of inputs would have the combined effect of lowering production costs and increasing the likelihood of collecting indemnities.

In short, the difficulties of accurately defining production costs make such cost-of-production programs highly suspect. It is unlikely that a workable definition of costs of production that would be representative of a range of farms could be constructed. Measurement of individual farms' costs of production would require very detailed farm records. Such records are simply not available in most areas.[3] Even for farms with such records, like the farms in the Kansas Farm Management Association, those records do not currently exist for individual crops. Finally, proposals that allow coverage levels to increase throughout the growing season are especially prone to moral hazard, since loss reporting could be delayed until late in the season when payouts are maximized.

Whole Farm Insurance

Insurance contracts that consider yield shortfalls among several crops are possible alternatives to the current program that treats contracts for individual crops separately. Revenue insurance is an extreme example of such insurance, whereby revenues from all crop enterprises are considered when determining losses and indemnities. A form of insurance that lies between individual crop coverage

3. In countries in which cost-of-production insurance programs have been introduced, as is noted below, indemnities have not been triggered when revenues fall below some estimates of a farm's costs of production but when revenues fall below the farm's operating loan; that is, in reality, those countries have not offered cost-of-production insurance but short-term credit insurance. This fact appears to have escaped the notice of many U.S. proponents of cost-of-production insurance.

and revenue insurance could be constructed. Such insurance could consider yields for a combination of crops or, alternatively, for all crops grown on a farm. This approach to insurance recognizes that yield outcomes among several crops on a farm may not be independent of one another (Atwood and Watts 1994).

To the extent that adverse growing conditions at times throughout the season may affect the various crops grown on a farm differently, additional information about yield outcomes might be obtained from a joint consideration of the crops. That is, more accurate premiums could possibly be constructed when the relationships among yields are considered.[4] Further, fixed administrative cost advantages might exist for contracts that evaluate all enterprises on a farm.

Many types of whole-farm or partial-farm insurance contracts are imaginable. In general, these contracts face the same limitations of defining expected yields as do existing insurance contracts. The increased complexity of whole-farm contract design may also limit the feasibility of such alternatives. In light of the difficulties of defining risks and appropriate premiums under the current program, workable whole-farm contracts are unlikely to be introduced in the near future. Current moves toward revenue insurance, however, may make some abbreviated form of whole-farm or revenue insurance relevant to policy debates in coming years.

Rainfall Insurance

Another form of insurance, patterned after contracts considered but not implemented in Australia, is rainfall in-

---

4. Atwood and Watts (1994), using data for farms growing corn and soybeans in Iowa, show that premiums for contracts that ensure a given minimum level of revenue to a farm can be much lower when the farm insures both crops and the correlation between yields across crops is correctly reflected in the contract premium.

surance. Proposals have included the formation of a rainfall futures contract and an area-yield insurance contract in which indemnities would be triggered when annual rainfall dropped below a predetermined level. Rainfall insurance proposals are simply area-yield insurance contracts in disguise and, as such, possess all the shortcomings of area-yield contracts. Area-yield contracts do not always offer farms protection when they suffer individual losses (Miranda 1991; Smith et al. 1994). Rainfall contracts tend to suffer even more severely from such problems because areas may experience losses even when annual rainfall appears to be adequate, partly because the timing of rainfall is often critical and partly because rainfall is never the only potential source of crop failure.

In his analysis of the willingness of Mallee River wheat producers to pay for insurance, Patrick (1988) found that such farmers value rainfall contracts much less than they value individual multiple-peril contracts, which, as we have noted above, were almost certainly not commercially viable. Patrick's results suggest that the farm lobby would have little interest in such contracts (especially with the diversity of sources of crop loss in the United States) unless they were heavily subsidized. Given these considerations, rainfall insurance proposals are unlikely to garner much support among policy makers.

Experience of Other Countries

In addition to other yield-based crop insurance schemes, several of the recent proposals to provide minimum guarantees for individual farm incomes (including cost-of-production and revenue insurance) have been implemented in other countries. The experiences of those countries provide some insights into the problems associated with such schemes. Several cross-country reviews of agricultural insurance plans exist in the literature on crop insurance

(Crawford 1977; Hazell, Pomerada, and Valdes 1986; Wright and Hewitt 1994). Here we draw on the evidence of those reviews and from the recent Canadian experience with revenue insurance to illuminate the problems of each scheme and their likely costs to taxpayers. The evidence is discouraging. Hazell et al. concluded from their survey of the literature that:

> The fact is that, with few exceptions, farmers in both developed and developing countries have been unwilling to pay the full cost of all-risk crop insurance....Consequently, most all-risk programs remain public sector schemes. Their management is often subject to political pressure regarding premiums and coverage and the programs are often used as a mechanism to transfer income to farmers. (Hazell et al. 1986, 7)

Wright and Hewitt arrived at a somewhat similar conclusion, arguing that:

> The main reason for the failure of all-risk insurance to meet expectations is that these expectations are explicitly or implicitly based on a theoretical model that overstates the potential value of such insurance. (Wright and Hewitt 1994, 106)

The expectations to which Wright and Hewitt refer concern, of course, the ability of such programs to provide protection to most farmers at zero or very low costs to taxpayers. The evidence presented below provides a ringing endorsement of the general conclusions of Hazell et al. and Wright and Hewitt.

The first question concerns the record of individual yield all-risk or multiple-peril insurance programs. Countries or regions of countries that have implemented such programs include Japan, Kenya, Mauritius, Mexico, Panama, and Sri Lanka and the states of Sao Paulo and Minas Gerais in Brazil. The individual-yield insurance programs provided by these countries and states differ in many respects, but they have one common important feature: payments are (or, in the case of Kenya's discontinued insurance program, were) triggered by a shortfall of the individual farm's actual crop yields relative to predetermined trigger values for those yields. In some countries, the participation of farmers in the insurance program has been compulsory for all farms of any reasonable size (Kenya, Japan, Mauritius, and Sri Lanka); in the others, participation has been compulsory only for farms with debt owed to government lending institutions and voluntary for farmers without such debt (Sao Paulo and Minas Gerais in Brazil and Mexico and Panama).

As Pomerada (1986) has emphasized, a primary goal of crop insurance in many countries has been to provide lending institutions with protection against defaults on agricultural loans to individual farmers. Thus, in some countries, coverage has been provided either for only the amount of the farmer's loan (Panama) or for the farm's "direct investment" at the time of the loss, which typically reflects the farmer's current operating loan (Mexico and the states of Sao Paulo and Minas Gerais in Brazil).[5] In addition, in some cases, indemnities for losses have been paid directly to the lending institution rather than to the farmer (for example, in Kenya, Mexico, Panama, and Sri Lanka).

In general, government-supported individual yield crop insurance programs have proved to be extremely

5. The programs offered by these countries have been described as "cost-of-production" insurance schemes but in fact do not provide coverage related to the farm's actual costs of production but to the farm's indebtedness, which can be measured very easily.

expensive to taxpayers and other sectors of the economy.[6] Typically, loss ratios have exceeded 1 (Wright and Hewitt 1994) and in some cases have been consistently large. The Kenya program, for example, operated an average loss ratio of about 5 over the period 1969–1974 (Crawford 1977), the Sao Paulo program experienced a cumulative loss ratio of about 1.6 over the period 1970–1980 (Lopes and Dias 1986), the Minas Gerais program experienced a cumulative loss ratio of 2.53 over the period 1973–1979 (Lopes and Dias), the Sri Lanka program experienced a cumulative loss ratio of about 3.5 over the period 1961–1973 (Crawford 1977), in the 1980s the Mexican program included subsidies for premiums that exceeded 50 percent of the actuarially sound premium rates (Bassoco et al. 1986), and throughout its entire history (from 1939 to 1994), the Japanese program has required premium subsidies in excess of 50 percent (Yamauchi 1986; FAO 1992).

The crop insurance programs in Mauritius and Panama generally operated with loss ratios of less than 1. The Mauritius crop insurance program is atypical in two important respects. First, the program has provided crop insurance for only one commodity—sugar cane—since its inception in 1948. Second, payments to individual farmers are made only if they are located in a region declared a disaster area because of drought or cyclones. Thus, payments to individual farmers have to be triggered by easily measured specific perils. One interesting aspect of the Mauritius program has been the difference between the loss ratios for relatively large plantation farms and for small farms. During the period 1961–1973, large farms experienced loss ratios of about 0.6, while small farms experienced loss ratios of about 1.04 (Crawford 1977). Clearly,

---

6. In some of these countries (for example, Brazil), losses have been funded through money creation rather than from tax revenues or government borrowing. The resulting inflation has therefore imposed the costs of the programs on the broadest possible spectrum of citizens.

at least during some periods, this insurance scheme has been administered to redistribute income from large to small farms (Crawford 1977; Wright and Hewitt 1994). In the case of Panama, while the loss ratio of the crop insurance program has been less than 1 in most of the years in which it has operated, as Wright and Hewitt pointed out, occasionally loss ratios have been large (for example, in 1982). In addition, the scope of the program has been relatively modest (Pomerada 1986).

The international evidence with respect to individual-yield crop insurance programs is, then, unambiguous. No country has managed to operate such a program on an actuarially sound basis for a wide variety of crops on a national scale. If, at least in this respect, government-sponsored individual-yield programs have been a bust, what about area-yield and revenue insurance programs? Government-supported area-yield crop insurance programs have been operated in India (since 1985) and in Sweden (from 1961 to 1988). All-risk revenue insurance programs have been offered in Brazil and in Canada. None of these programs has proved to be an actuarial success.

India did not have a crop insurance program for its farmers until 1985, although between 1947 and 1985 many such programs were seriously considered by successive governments (Crawford 1977; Sen 1987). Given the magnitude of the budgetary costs of the program between 1986 and 1991, perhaps earlier governments showed good judgment by refusing to introduce such programs. The main objective of area-yield crop insurance programs has been to remove incentives for moral-hazard behavior on the part of individual farmers, thereby reducing losses and indemnities. Although adverse selection may be a problem for area-yield programs because of errors in rate setting across regions, an area-yield program can still be an actuarial disaster even if, as is the case with the Indian program, compulsory participation precludes adverse-selection problems. All the insurer has to do is to set the premium rates too low. This is clearly what has happened in the Indian program. Between 1986 and 1990, the lowest annual loss ratio for the program was 2.16, in the worst year (1988) the loss ratio exceeded 10, and the cumulative loss ratio over the entire five-year period was 6.86. Wright and Hewitt noted that such an actuarial outcome would not be a surprise. Before the introduction of the national program, the Indian government deliberately cut premiums rates by 50 percent from levels that had proved to be approximately actuarially sound in an earlier pilot program to make the compulsory program politically acceptable to a majority of farmers.

Sweden's fiscal experience with government-sponsored area-yield contracts from 1961 to 1988 was not much better. By design, the Swedish program included a 100 percent subsidy for all administrative costs of the program and a 66 percent subsidy of all expected indemnities. Inevitably, loss ratios were typically large (Crawford 1977; Wright and Hewitt 1994). In 1988, confronted with serious general budgetary problems, the Swedish government decided to reduce its program subsidies to about 20 percent of expected indemnities and to require that some administrative costs be paid by farmers. Evidence on loss ratios for recent years is not available.

All-risk revenue insurance programs have been implemented in Brazil and in Canada. The Brazilian program, PROAGRO, was intended to be a short-term credit insurance program (Lopes and Dias 1986) and was compulsory for all crop and livestock farmers with financing from the Brazilian National System of Agricultural Credit. Under PROAGRO, farmers received indemnities when farm revenue fell below the amount required for repayment of the farm's loan from the agricultural credit system. Indemnities, therefore, were triggered by revenue shortfalls and not just by crop yield shortfalls. The actuarial performance of the scheme was poor. Over the period 1976–1980, the annual loss ratio was less than 1 in only one year (1978), and the cumulative loss ratio for the program was about 1.2 (Lopes and Dias). In general, although the program was limited in scope (available only to farms with a specific source of debt) and care was taken in adjusting losses (Lopes and Dias), the Brazilian revenue insurance program was not operated in an actuarially sound manner.

The current Canadian crop insurance program is extremely complex. Each of the nine Canadian provinces has been permitted to develop its own program for providing farmers with either crop insurance, revenue insurance, or both.[7] The origins of the current melange of programs are as follows. In the early 1920s, an initial attempt by a private insurance company to offer all-risk crop insurance in the Canadian prairie provinces proved an actuarial disaster. Subsequently, under the 1939 Prairie Assistance Act, a permanent disaster relief fund was established via a 1 percent levy on grain sales (Elrifi 1991). After several disasters in the 1950s, producers became dissatisfied with the program, and, as a result, national all-risk or multiple-peril crop insurance program was first introduced in Canada through the 1959 Federal Crop Insurance Act (Elrifi). The pure crop insurance program proved expensive. Despite a large federal premium subsidy, premiums (including both government and farmer contributions) were in general about 20 percent smaller than indemnities during the 1970s and 1980s (Elrifi). A review of the program by Agriculture Canada in 1989 led to the Farm Income Protection Act of 1991, which introduced a federal mandate for province-specific revenue insurance plans (Turvey and Chen 1994).

Under this federal mandate, the nine Canadian provinces have implemented five types of revenue insurance

7. Turvey and Chen (1994) provide one of the more useful guides through the labyrinth of Canadian crop and revenue insurance programs. Elrifi (1991) describes the legal histroy of Canadian crop insurance programs and discusses the implications of case law for current programs.

programs for crop producers. Turvey and Chen have categorized the programs as follows:

- pure revenue insurance under the Gross Revenue Insurance Program offered by Novia Scotia and Prince Edward Island
- a mixture of gross revenue insurance and crop insurance offered by British Columbia, Alberta, Manitoba, and New Brunswick
- a combination of market revenue insurance and crop insurance offered by Ontario
- all-crop area-based revenue insurance offered by Saskatchewan
- commodity-specific area-based revenue insurance offered by Quebec

The first three programs provide individual farmers with indemnities based on their own crop yield and revenue experience. The last two programs provide farmers with indemnities based on area revenue shortfalls and are thus similar to area-yield programs.

Over the period 1991–1994, in aggregate, despite built-in premium subsidies, these revenue insurance programs operated at a loss, and indemnities exceeded total premiums (including both government and farmer contributions) by about 3.3 percent. The aggregate figures hide an interesting trend. Initially, target revenues were set at relatively high levels because the estimated market prices on which target revenues were based were computed on a fifteen-year moving average. In 1991 and 1992, therefore, this market price average included some abnormally high-price years from the mid-1970s. The upshot was that indemnities were large during the first two years of the program but declined sharply in 1993. At the same time, because of large losses in the first two years and a mandate that premiums (inclusive of planned government subsidies) be self-funding over a five-year period, premium rates were increased quite substantially (Turvey and

Chen 1994). The higher premium rates and lower indemnities were successful in generating a loss ratio of less than 1 in 1993 but at an important political cost; farmer participation rates fell sharply, raising substantive questions about the political viability of the program.

The brief history of revenue insurance in Canada captures, in many respects, the experiences of most all-risk crop insurance programs. Program success, in terms of participation, is achieved only when subsidies are large. When policy makers introduce measures to reduce subsidies (and loss ratios), participation falls; the programs become politically unpopular with farmers, the client group they are intended to benefit; and the programs fail to capture votes and other types of support for the politicians who have been their advocates. The programs then either die (as was the case in Kenya) or are revised to encourage greater participation (as has been the recent case in the United States), but almost surely improved participation comes only at the cost of higher subsidies.

7
Conclusion

In the introduction to this monograph, we raised two fundamentally important questions about disaster relief and crop insurance programs. First, is there any meaningful economic rationale for such programs? Second, if for political economy or other reasons such programs have to be a part of U.S. farm policy, what characteristics should be incorporated to make them as efficient as possible?

Arguments for Subsidies

As far as we can tell, no substantial technical economic efficiency arguments justify government subsidies for either agricultural insurance or disaster relief programs in a highly diversified, financially sophisticated economy like that of the United States. One potential argument for such intervention is that private insurance companies are unable to diversify systemic risks like those endemic to crop production. In chapter 4, we pointed out that, while an individual insurance company specializing in agriculture may face systemic risks, such a company always has access to reinsurance markets such as Lloyd's of London in which other companies and individuals specialize in risk diversification services. If the risks of satellite and space shuttle launches can be diversified in such markets, so too can crop losses and other agricultural risks. Thus, the argument that the existence of systemic risk is prima facie evidence of market failure with respect to crop insurance does not appear to be particularly credible.

The only justification for government intervention in this case would be that government can diversify such risks more efficiently than private reinsurance. No one has seriously tried to make that case, however. Certainly, private reinsurers provide their services at a cost, but unless we have a compelling reason to believe that the supply side of the reinsurance market exhibits a considerable degree of imperfect competition or even monopoly, we have no reason to suppose that a government agency could do the same job at a lower cost.

A second argument for government intervention, also examined in chapter 4, is that moral hazard and adverse selection are sources of market failure in the market for crop insurance and that the government should therefore step in to operate welfare-enhancing crop insurance programs. Certainly, as we pointed out in chapter 5, there is considerable evidence of both adverse selection and moral hazard in the current federal MPCI program. Adverse selection, however, is a direct consequence of inappropriate procedures for setting premium rates. No evidence suggests that governments, either in the United States or elsewhere, are better at setting premium rates than private reinsurance companies. In fact, as we pointed out in chapter 2, to avoid political confrontations, the FCIC has deliberately used rate-setting procedures that smooth premium rates across counties and within entire states in a way that encourages adverse selection. It is hard to imagine that private insurers would select such a strategy.

Clearly, as we also discussed in chapter 4, results from economic theory indicate that potential moral-hazard effects may preclude a private market for all-risk multiple-peril crop insurance. Some of these effects could be mitigated by contract design (for example, through multiyear contracts with substantial penalties for cheating or contracts with large deductibles). Governments are unlikely to be in a better position than a competitive private insurance industry to develop the flexible portfolio of insurance contracts for resolving moral-hazard problems in an optimal manner. Moral hazard, however, is not a technical market failure but a market condition that may simply be too costly to mitigate. Again, the only reasonable argument for government intervention on these grounds would be that the government, because of better information, can monitor farm behavior more accurately or more cheaply than can private insurers. This proposition is not compelling either. Private insurers have strong profit incentives to mitigate moral-hazard problems. Policy makers are often more concerned with ensuring that politically influential groups such as the farm lobby are satisfied with crop insurance programs than with ensuring that the programs are reasonably free of moral hazard.

A third quasi-technical argument for some kind of federal disaster or crop insurance program is quite simply that farmers want and are willing to pay for protection against price and production risk but that the private market simply refuses to supply much-needed all-risk insurance contracts, for whatever reason. The proponents presumably mean that some kind of market failure exists prohibiting the development of an otherwise welfare-enhancing product. The empirical evidence reviewed in chapter 5, however, indicates that while some (perhaps many) farmers are willing to pay premiums in excess of expected returns to accomplish income smoothing through insurance contracts, they are not willing to pay very much (Bardsley et al. 1984; Fraser 1988; Patrick 1988).

Certainly, most farmers do not appear willing to pay enough for such services to cover the normal loading factors required by competitive insurance companies to cover their costs of doing business. In other words, the risk-reduction services provided by multiple-peril crop insurance contracts are not worth a great deal to most farmers, probably because they have so many other ways of managing the risk associated with agricultural income streams (through geographic and enterprise diversification, input-use management, off-farm income, and the like). When products are not worth very much to consumers and are quite costly to produce (as is the case with covered wagons in the transport industry of the 1990s), the private market does not supply those products because they are worth less to consumers than they cost to make. All-risk crop insurance is possibly one such product.

If market failure arguments are not particularly plausible rationales for government intervention in crop insurance markets, what about equity considerations? As we discussed in chapter 3, concerns about low and highly variable incomes in the farm sector during the mid-1930s played a role in the development of the original U.S. federal crop insurance program. Then, on average, farm households had much lower money incomes and wealth than did nonfarm households, and it is by no means implausible that insurance and disaster relief programs could be justified by humanitarian concern. It is no longer obvious, however, that on average farm households are economically disadvantaged (Pasour 1990). Thus, in general, equity concerns should not be dominant in debates over farm subsidy disaster relief and crop insurance programs. In fact, the current heavily subsidized U.S. crop insurance program has very little to recommend it as an income redistribution program. Farms face no limits on the value of the crops against which they can purchase subsidized insurance, and thus indemnities and subsidies are largely proportional to farm size and farm income. The program makes no pretense of providing larger premium subsidies to farm households with low incomes; it simply provides much larger absolute subsidies to larger operations.

Purpose of Crop Insurance

If crop insurance programs serve no obvious purpose in improving economic efficiency and have little to recommend them with respect to reasonable concerns about equity and social justice, then why do they exist? The answer may be that they are politically palatable ways of transferring income to an effective interest group. Farmers, after all, do provide essential commodities that sustain life, and their production is more subject to chance events than that of most other industries. In years when disasters hit, they also receive below-average incomes. Thus in low-income years voters and taxpayers may be more willing to tolerate income transfers to farmers through such programs as all-risk crop insurance and disaster aid. As we pointed out in chapter 3, political expediency was a crucial component in the development of the 1938 Federal Crop Insurance Act; political expediency may well continue to ensure that some form of disaster aid program continues for many years.

If disaster aid programs are to continue, at least they should be structured to minimize the costs of providing the benefits they supply to farmers. We begin with the presumption that the costs to taxpayers of such programs will be greater than the revenues they generate in the form of premiums. As we showed in chapter 6, almost no country has managed to operate any form of agricultural insurance program without large subsidies unless they have been willing to accept very low participation rates. In the United States, during the period 1956–1980 in which loss ratios were close to 1, participation was very modest (less than 10 percent of insurable acres was covered). During the 1980s and early 1990s, participation rates have increased somewhat (to between 20 and 40 percent of insurable acres) but only because subsidies have increased and loss ratios have been close to 2. Although some observers have argued that premium rates have little effect on participation, their position is not supported by the empirical evidence reviewed in chapter 5. Lowering premium rates through increased subsidies is a viable method for increasing participation—the only problem is that because demand is affected by adverse selection, lowering premiums may also increase loss ratios.

A second reasonable presumption is that a disaster aid program should provide protection to as many farms as possible for any given level of subsidies. One way of accomplishing this goal is to ensure that premium rates are set in a way that minimizes adverse-selection effects. If aid is to be provided through a crop insurance program, premiums should be established at the farm level using methods that reflect the farm's actual risk of loss. Thus, rate-setting procedures that smooth premium rates across adjacent counties and across counties within states should be abandoned, as should procedures that ignore information about variability in individual farm yields. Severe adverse selection can be avoided only if premium rates reflect the farm's risk of loss fairly accurately, but such rates can be established only if farms provide meaningful data on historical yields. Any legislation should therefore provide substantial incentives for farms to provide accurate data. These types of incentives are incorporated in the provisions of the 1994 Crop Insurance Reform Act, which imposes heavy penalties on farmers who fail to provide historical yield data or who practice fraud.

Alternatives to Present Programs

Incentives for actuarial soundness are also likely to be much greater when insurance services are provided by private markets than by government bureaucracies. Barnaby (1994), for example, has pointed out that revenue insurance can be provided through the use of government-reinsured MPCI contracts, replacement contracts, and target price puts sold in private financial markets. Miranda and Glauber (1994) have suggested privately traded area-yield contracts as a low-cost vehicle for allowing crop insurance companies to reinsure against systemic risk. These initiatives may be useful vehicles for minimizing subsidies and allowing taxpayer contributions to farm wealth to be used more effectively.

Area-yield insurance contracts have been proposed as an alternative to providing farmers with protection against yield risks that avoids moral-hazard problems. The difficulty with such contracts is that, for any given premium outlay, they afford the average farmer with less reduction of risk and are therefore less valuable. In other words, even if the moral-hazard effects of individual contracts are small, farmers will buy area-yield contracts rather than individual-yield contracts only if the subsidies built into area-yield premiums are larger than the subsidies built into individual-yield contracts. If the moral-hazard effects of individual-yield contracts are large, the premium subsidies required to make area-yield contracts attractive to farmers will have to be much larger. From the perspective of political economy, then, area-yield insurance is probably not politically viable as a national disaster aid program because, if the subsidy is low, farmers will not be interested in area-yield contracts and if it is transparently high (as was the case in Sweden), taxpayers may object. Nevertheless, a useful political purpose may be served by area-yield insurance in relation to crops for which moral-hazard risks preclude any type of individual-yield contract. Such crops include many fruits and vegetables, for example, lettuce and asparagus. If the Federal Crop Insurance Corporation is required to provide insurance for all crops and all producers, area-yield contracts could be offered for such minor crops (often for areas larger than counties) that would turn into major actuarial disasters under an individual-yield multiple-peril program.

What about the revenue assurance or insurance and cost-of-production programs discussed by policy makers? Cost-of-production insurance under which each farm receives coverage based on its unmeasurable costs of production is an unworkable concept. The government might equally well approach small shopkeepers and promise them that they would never go broke because the government would always guarantee them an income sufficient to cover any expenses they might choose to incur. Credit insurance is a more feasible version of this type of contract, at least from the perspective of its implementation, because the indemnity trigger is easier to measure. Operating loans, however, are endogenous to the farm's operation, and therefore credit insurance is clearly subject to moral hazard. In fact, credit insurance (and other types of insurance) can lead to illicit collusion between lenders and borrowers. After all, if a lender knows that a loan to a farm is insured, what incentive does the lender have to make prudent loans or expend much effort in encouraging borrowers in default to make interest or principal payments? In some respects, this type of insurance is a road well-traveled by government regulators and at its end sometimes lie unpleasant analogs to the savings and loan debacle of the 1980s.

While revenue insurance or assurance is appealing to some farmers, at least in Iowa, the implementation of such a program is fraught with difficulties. Under a revenue insurance plan, setting insurance premiums for each farm is likely to prove an actuarial nightmare. Opportunities for moral hazard and outright fraud are also likely to be legion under such a contract. A revenue assurance program would face identical moral-hazard and fraud problems since the only difference between revenue insurance and revenue assurance is that the latter is free. It is noteworthy that provinces like Saskatchewan in Canada that offer whole farm multicrop revenue insurance do so only in the context of area-yield insurance. They do not offer each farm a revenue contract based on its individual portfolio of crops under which indemnities are triggered by its own revenue shortfalls.

Finally, what is really required with respect to agricultural disaster aid or crop insurance programs? Farmers on average are not poor. They have a plethora of tools for managing production risk through input-use choices, geographic and enterprise diversification, and the direct and indirect use of futures markets to hedge against unanticipated price movements. The agricultural sector in the United States is not, fundamentally, much different from many other sectors that face risk. In that context, if agricultural insurance products are not commercially viable because the buyers do not value them at what they cost to produce, then the government or members of society have no major reason to be worried about whether they exist.

If, as seems to be the case, political expediency dictates that disaster aid be provided to the farm sector, then some form of crop insurance program in which premiums and premium subsidies are determined in an actuarially sensible fashion is almost certainly a much better deal than ad hoc disaster relief bills. To that end, the provisions of the 1994 Crop Insurance Reform Act that, to some extent, tie Congress's hands with respect to the passage of ad hoc disaster bills are worthwhile. No legislation has any hope of limiting insurance program subsidies, however, if short-term political agendas determine premium rates rather than long-term actuarial principles that use reasonably accurate data about individual farm yields.

References

Agricultural Stabilization and Conservation Service, U.S. Department of Agriculture. *Disaster Relief Statistics,* 1994.

Akerlof, G. "The Market for 'Lemons': Qualitative Uncertainty and the Market Mechanism." *Quarterly Journal of Economics* 89(1970): 488–500.

Alston, J. M., C. A. Carter, and V. H. Smith. "Rationalizing Agricultural Export Subsidies." *American Journal of Agricultural Economics* 75(1993):1000–10.

Alston, J. M., and B. H. Hurd. "Some Neglected Social Costs of Government Spending on Farm Programs." *American Journal of Agricultural Economics* 72(1990):149–56.

Arrow, K. "Uncertainty and the Welfare Economics of Medical Care." *American Economic Review* 53(1963):941–73.

Atwood, J. A., and M. J. Watts. "Creating a Crop Portfolio Insurance Policy." Unpublished manuscript, Montana State University, 1994.

Baquet, A. E., and J. R. Skees. "Group Risk Plan Insurance: An Alternative Risk Management Tool for Farmers." *Choices* (First quarter, 1994):25–28.

Bardsley, P., A. Abbey, and S. Davenport. "The Economics of Insuring Crops against Drought." *Australian Journal of Agricultural Economics* 28(1984):1–14.

Barnaby, G. A. "Using Private Markets to Achieve Revenue Insurance." Paper presented at the AAEA Risk Management Preconference, San Diego, California, August 6, 1994.

Barnaby, G. A., and J. Skees. "Public Policy for Catastrophic Yield Risk: An Alternative Crop Insurance Program." *Choices* (Second quarter 1990):7–9.

Barnett, B. J. and J. R. Skees. "An Empirical Analysis of the Demand for Crop Insurance: Comment." *American Journal of Agricultural Economics,* forthcoming, November 1994.

Barnett, B. J., J. R. Skees, and J. D. Hourigan. "Examining Participation in Federal Crop Insurance." Staff paper no. 275, Department of Agricultural Economics, University of Kentucky, August 1990.

Bassoco, L. M., C. Cartis, and R. D. Norton. "Sectoral Analysis of the Benefits of Subsidized Insurance in Mexico." In *Crop Insurance for Agricultural Development: Issues and Experience,* edited by P. Hazell, C. Pomerada, and A. Valdes. Baltimore: Johns Hopkins University Press, 1986.

Becker, G. S. "A Theory of Competition among Pressure Groups for Political Influence." *Quarterly Journal of Economics* 68(1983):371–400.

Beeson, B. E. "Management of Insurable Risk by East Tennessee Tobacco Farmers." Ph.D. diss., University of Tennessee, 1971.

Blandford, D., H. DeGorter, B. Gardner, and D. Harvey. "There Is a Way to Support Farm Income with Minimal Trade Distortions." *Choices* (1990):20–25.

Borch, K. H. "The Safety Loading of Reinsurance Premiums." *Skandinavisk Aktuarietidskrift* (1962): 162–75.

————. "The Monster in Loch Ness." *Journal of Risk and Insurance* 33(1982a):521-25.

————. "Insuring and Auditing the Auditor." In *Games Economics Dynamics and Time Series Analysis*, edited by Diestler, Fürst, and Schüdianer. Physica Verdag, 1982b.

————. *Economics of Insurance*. Amsterdam: North Holland, 1989.

Botts, R. R. "Experience with Wheat and Cotton Crop Insurance." *Agricultural Finance Review* 6(1943):31.

Botts, R. R., and J. N. Boles. "Use of Normal-Curve Theory in Crop Insurance Rate Making." *Journal of Farm Economics* 39(1957):733–40.

Bray, N. R. "Performance of Federal Crop Insurance in Western Nebraska." Master's thesis, University of Nebraska, 1963.

Bullock, D. S. "What Political Preference Studies Measure and Assume." *American Journal of Agricultural Economics* 76(1994):247–361.

Calvin, L. "Participation in Federal Crop Insurance." Paper presented at the Southern Agricultural Economics Association, Little Rock, Arkansas, 1990.

Chambers, R. G. "Insurability and Moral Hazard in Agricultural Insurance Markets." *American Journal of Agricultural Economics* 71(1989):604–16.

Clendenin, T. C. "Federal Crop Insurance in Operation." *Wheat Studies of the Food Research Institute* 18(1942):232.

Coble, K. H., T. O. Knight, R. D. Pope, and J. R. Williams. "An Empirical Test for Moral Hazard and Adverse Selection in Multiple Peril Crop Insurance." Paper presented at the annual meeting of the American Agricultural Economics Association, Orlando, Florida, August 1993.

Crawford, P. R. "Crop Insurance in Developing Countries: A Critical Approach." Master's thesis, University of Wisconsin, Madison, 1977.

Elrifi, I. "A Comparison of Crop Insurance in the United States and Canada." *Journal of Agricultural Taxation and Law* 2(1991):99–133.

Food and Agricultural Organization. *Crop Insurance Compendium: 1991.* Rome: FAO, 1992.

Fraser, R. W. "A Method for Evaluating Supply Response to Price Uncertainty." *Australian Journal of Agricultural Economics* 32(1988):22–36.

Freund, R. J. "The Introduction of Risk into a Programming Model." *Econometrica* 24(1956):253–63.

Gantz, Eugene. "GRP—Sounds like Socialism." *Choices* (Third quarter 1994): 45.

Gardner, B. L. "The Farmers' Risk and Financial Environment under the Food and Agriculture Act of 1977." *Agricultural Finance Review* 39(1979):123–91.

———. "Efficient Redistribution through Commodity Markets." *American Journal of Agricultural Economics* 65(1983):325–34.

———. "Causes of Farm Commodity Programs." *Journal of Political Economy* 95(1987):290–310.

———. "Export Policy, Deficiency Payments, and a Consumption Tax." *Journal of Agricultural Economics Research* 40(Winter 1988):38–41.

Gardner, B. L., and R. A. Kramer. "Experience with Crop Insurance Programs in the United States." In *Crop Insurance for Agricultural Development: Issues and Experience,* edited by P. Hazell, C. Pomerada, and A. Valdez, 195–222. Baltimore: Johns Hopkins University Press, 1986.

Goodwin, B. K. "An Empirical Analysis of the Demand for Multiple Peril Crop Insurance." *American Journal of Agricultural Economics* 75(May 1993):425–34.

———. "Semiparametric (Distribution-Free) Evaluation of Discrete Choice under Uncertainty: Adverse Selection, Disaster Relief, and the Demand for Insurance."

Unpublished manuscript, Department of Agricultural and Resource Economics, North Carolina State University, 1994.

Goodwin, B. K., and T. L. Kastens. "Adverse Selection, Disaster Relief, and the Demand for Multiple Peril Crop Insurance." Research report to the Federal Crop Insurance Corporation, Kansas State University, 1993.

Goodwin, B. K., and A. P. Ker. "An Evaluation of Current Rating and Yield Forecasting Procedures in the Group Risk (GRP) Federal Crop Insurance Program." Research report to the Federal Crop Insurance Corporation, Department of Agricultural and Resource Economics, North Carolina State University, 1994.

Halcrow, H. G. "Actuarial Structures for Crop Insurance." *Journal of Farm Economics* 31(1949):418–43.

Harrington, D. H., and O. C. Doering III. "Agricultural Policy Reform: A Proposal." *Choices* (First quarter 1993).

Hartman, R. S. "A Note on the Use of Aggregate Data in Individual Choice Models." *Journal of Econometrics* 18(1982):313–35.

———. "The Estimation of Short Run Household Electricity Demand Using Pooled Aggregate Data." *Journal of Business and Economic Statistics* 1(1983):127–35.

Hazell, P., C. Pomerada, and A. Valdes. *Crop Insurance for Agricultural Development: Issues and Experience.* Baltimore: Johns Hopkins University Press, 1986.

Hoffman, W. L., C. Campbell, and K. A. Cook. *Sowing Disaster: The Implications of Farm Disaster Programs for Taxpayers and the Environment.* Washington, D.C.: Environmental Working Group, 1994.

Hojjati, B., and N. E. Bockstael. "Modeling the Demand for Crop Insurance." In *Multiple Peril Crop Insurance: A Collection of Empirical Studies,* edited by H. Mapp, 153–76. Southern Cooperative Series bulletin no. 334, May 1988.

Horowitz, J. K., and E. Lichtenberg. "Insurance, Moral Hazard, and Chemical Use in Agriculture." *American Journal of Agricultural Economics* 75(1993):926–35.

Interagency Floodplain Management Review Committee. *Sharing the Challenge: Floodplain Management into the 21st Century.* Washington, D.C., 1994.

Iowa Farm Bill Study Team. "The Findings of the 1995 Farm Bill Study Team." Unpublished manuscript, Iowa Farm Bureau, 1994.

Jones, L. A., and D. K. Larson. *Economic Impact of Federal Crop Insurance in Selected Areas of Virginia and Montana.* Agricultural Economics Report no. 75, Washington, D.C.: U.S. Department of Agriculture, 1965.

Just, R. E., and L. Calvin. "An Empirical Analysis of U.S. Participation in Crop Insurance." Paper prepared for the University of Maryland/Saskatchewan Conference for the Improvement of Agricultural Crop Insurance, April 1–3, 1990, Regina, Saskatchewan.

Kahneman, D., and A. Tversky. "Prospect Theory: An Analysis of Decision under Risk." *Econometrica* 50(1979):263–91.

Knight, F. H. *Risk, Uncertainty, and Profit.* New York: Harper and Row Publishers, 1921 (reprinted 1965).

Kramer, R. A. "Federal Crop Insurance: 1938–1982." *Agricultural History* 57 (1983):181-200.

Laffont, J. J. *The Economics of Uncertainty and Information.* Cambridge, Mass.: MIT Press, 1989.

Lambert, R. "Long Term Contracts and Moral Hazard." *Bell Journal of Economics* 14(1983):441–52.

Layard, P. R. G., and A. A. Walters. *Microeconomic Theory.* New York: McGraw-Hill, 1978.

Leppert, N., and R. McIlwain. "1993 Midwest Flood: Summary of USDA Assistance." USDA, FmHA, and ASCS unpublished bulletin, June 13, 1994.

Loftsgard, L. D. "Attitudinal Reactions to the FCIC Program." In *Crop Insurance in the Great Plains.* Bozeman,

Montana: Montana Agricultural Experiment Station, bulletin no. 617, 1967.

Lopes, M. de R., and G. L. de Salra Dias. "The Brazilian Experience and Crop Insurance Programs." In *Crop Insurance for Agricultural Development: Issues and Experience,* edited by P. Hazell, C. Pomerada, and A. Valdes. Baltimore: Johns Hopkins University Press, 1986.

Miranda, M. J. "Area-Yield Crop Insurance Reconsidered." *American Journal of Agricultural Economics* May 73(1991):233–42.

Miranda, M. J., and J. Glauber. "Uninsurable Systemic Risk and the Future of Crop Insurance Markets: A Cure for Area Yield Options." Ohio State University Department of Agricultural Economics working paper, 1994.

Nelson, C. H., and E. T. Loehman. "Further toward a Theory of Agricultural Insurance." *American Journal of Agricultural Economics* 69(1987):523–31.

Neumann, J. von., and O. Morgenstern. *Theory of Games and Economic Behavior.* Princeton, N.J.: Princeton University Press, 1944.

Nieuwoudt, W. L., S. R. Johnson, A. W. Womack, and J. B. Bullock. "The Demand for Crop Insurance." Agricultural Economics Report no. 1985–16, Department of Agricultural Economics, University of Missouri, 1985.

Pasour, E. C. *Agriculture and the State: Market Processes and Bureaucracy.* New York: Holmes and Meier, 1990.

Patrick, G. F. "Mallee Wheat Farmers' Demand for Crop and Rainfall Insurance." *Australian Journal of Agricultural Economics* 32(1988):37–49.

Pomerada, C. "An Evaluation of the Impact of Credit Insurance on Bank Performance in Panama." In *Crop Insurance for Agricultural Development: Issues and Experience,* edited by P. Hazell, C. Pomerada, and A. Valdes. Baltimore: Johns Hopkins University Press, 1986.

Quiggin, J. "A Note on the Variability of Rainfall Insur-

141

ance." *Australian Journal of Agricultural Economics* 30(1986):63–69.

———. "The Optimal Design of Crop Insurance." In *Economics of Agricultural Crop Insurance: Theory and Evidence*, edited by D. L. Hueth and W. H. Furtan. Boston: Kluwer Academic Press, 1994.

Raviv, A. "The Design of an Optimal Insurance Policy." *American Economic Review* 69(1979):84–96.

Rogerson, W. "Repeated Moral Hazard." *Econometrics* 52(1985):69–76.

Rothschild, M., and J. Stiglitz. "Equilibrium in Competitive Insurance Markets." *Quarterly Journal of Economics* 26(1977):629–49.

Rubenstein, A., and M. Yaari. "Expected Insurance Contracts and Moral Hazard." *Journal of Economic Theory* 30(1983):74–97.

Sanderson, F. H. "A Specific Risk Scheme for Wheat Crop Insurance." *Journal of Farm Economics* 25(1943):759–76.

Sen, A. C. "India." In *Crop Insurance in Asia*. Tokyo: Asian Productivity Organization, 1987.

Shipley, J. "The Role of Federal Crop Insurance in a Changing Agriculture." *Crop Insurance in the Great Plains*. Bozeman, Montana: Montana Agricultural Experiment Station, bulletin no. 617, 1967.

Skees, J. R. "The Political Economy of a Crop Insurance Experiment." Paper delivered at the W. I. Myers Lecture, October 14, 1994, Cornell University.

Skees, J. R., and R. Black. "Rating the Group Risk Plan: A New FCIC Product." Unpublished manuscript, Department of Agricultural Economics, University of Kentucky, 1993.

Skees, J. R., and M. R. Reed. "Rate-making and Farm-Level Crop Insurance: Implications for Adverse Selection." *American Journal of Agricultural Economics* 68(1986):653–59.

Smith, Adam. *An Inquiry into the Wealth of Nations.* Indianapolis: Library Classics, 1981.

Smith, V. H., and A. E. Baquet. "The Demand for Multiple Peril Crop Insurance: Evidence from the Great Plains." *Montana Ag Research* (Spring 1993).

Smith, V. H., H. M. Chouinard, and A. E. Baquet. "Almost Ideal Area Yield Crop Insurance Contracts." *Agricultural and Resource Economics Review* (1994):75-83.

Smith, V. H., and B. K. Goodwin. "Crop Insurance, Moral Hazard, and Agricultural Chemical Use." Unpublished manuscript, Department of Economics, Montana State University, 1994.

Smith, V. H., and M. R. Kehoe. "The Economics of Marketing Multiple Peril Crop Insurance." Selected paper presented at the Annual Meeting of the American Agricultural Economics Association, San Diego, 1994.

Starr, G. D. "The Federal Crop Insurance Program in Eastern Nebraska: Saunders County, A Case Study." Master's thesis, University of Nebraska, 1963.

Turvey, C. G., and K. Chen. "Canadian Safety Net Programs for Agriculture." Paper presented at the Annual Meeting of the American Agricultural Economics Association, San Diego, 1994.

Tweeten, L., C. Zulauf, A. Lines, and G. Cramer. *Farm Revenue Assurance or Income Insurance.* Anderson Chair Publication, ESO 2132, Department of Agricultural Economics and Rural Sociology, Ohio State University, 1994.

U.S. General Accounting Office. "The Federal Crop Insurance Program Can Be Made More Effective." Washington, D.C., 1977.

————. "The Department of Agriculture Federal Crop Insurance Corporation," by Brian P. Crawley. In *Review of Federal Crop Insurance Program*, Hearing before the Subcommittee on Conservation, Credit, and Rural Development, Committee on Agriculture, House of Representatives. GAO Serial 98–7. Washington, D.C., November 1983.

———. "Crop Insurance: Overpayment of Claims by Private Companies Costs the Government Millions." Report to the chairman, Subcommittee on Conservation, Credit, and Rural Development, Committee on Agriculture, House of Representatives. GAO/RCED-88–7. Washington, D.C., 1987.

———. "Disaster Assistance: Crop Insurance Can Provide Assistance More Effectively Than Other Programs." Report to the chairman, Committee on Agriculture, House of Representatives. GAO/RCED-89-211. Washington, D.C., 1989.

———. "Crop Insurance: Program Has Not Fostered Significant Risk Sharing by Insurance Companies." GAO/RCED-92-25. Washington, D.C., January 1992.

———. "Crop Insurance: Federal Program Faces Insurability and Design Problems." GAO/RCED-93-98. Washington, D.C., May 1993.

Valgren, V. N. *Crop Insurance: Risks, Losses, and Principles of Protection.* USDA Bulletin 1043. Washington, D.C.: United States Department of Agriculture, 1923.

Vercammen, J., and G. C. Van Kooten. "Moral Hazard Cycles in Individual-Coverage Crop Insurance." *American Journal of Agricultural Economics* 76(1994):250-61.

Wright, B. D., and J. A. Hewitt. "All Risk Crop Insurance: Lessons from Theory and Experience." In *Economics of Agricultural Crop Insurance: Theory and Evidence,* edited by D. L. Hueth and W. H. Furtan. Boston: Kluwer Academic Publishers, 1994.

Yamauchi, T. "Evolution of the Crop Insurance Program in Japan." In *Crop Insurance for Agricultural Development: Issues and Experience,* edited by P. Hazell, C. Pomerada, and A. Valdes. Baltimore: Johns Hopkins University Press, 1986.

Zering, K. D., C. O. McCorkle, and C. V. Moon. "The Utility of Multiple Peril Crop Insurance for Irrigated, Multiple-Crop Agriculture." *Western Journal of Agricultural Economics* 12(1987):50–59.

Index

About the Authors

BARRY K. GOODWIN is associate professor in the Department of Agricultural and Resource Economics at North Carolina State University. He previously served as associate professor in the Department of Agricultural Economics at Kansas State University. Mr. Goodwin's work emphasizes agricultural policy and price analysis, international trade, and applied econometrics. He is the author of numerous articles, book chapters, and other publications on agricultural policy and international trade.

VINCENT H. SMITH is associate professor in the Department of Agricultural Economics and Economics at Montana State University. He has served as a consultant to the U.S. Environmental Protection Agency, a consultant to U.S. AID and the government of Tanzania on the consumption effect of agricultural policy in Tanzania, and an economist in the Energy and Environmental Research Division at the Department of Economics, Research Triangle Park Institute. Mr. Smith was on the faculties of Manchester University, North Carolina State University, Trinity College, and the University of Richmond. He is the author of several books, articles, and publications on agricultural and economic policy.

A NOTE ON THE BOOK

This book was edited by Dana Lane
of the publications staff
of the American Enterprise Institute.
The figures were drawn by Hördur Karlsson.
The index was prepared by Robert Elwood.
The text was set in Palatino, a typeface
designed by the twentieth-century Swiss designer
Hermann Zapf. Lisa Roman of the AEI Press
set the type, and Braun-Brumfield, Inc.,
of Ann Arbor, Michigan,
printed and bound the book,
using permanent acid-free paper.

The AEI Press is the publisher for the American Enterprise Institute for Public Policy Research, 1150 Seventeenth Street, N.W., Washington, D.C. 20036; *Christopher DeMuth,* publisher; *Dana Lane,* director; *Ann Petty,* editor; *Leigh Tripoli,* editor; *Cheryl Weissman,* editor; *Lisa Roman,* editorial assistant (rights and permissions).